Freedom
within a
framework

Freedom
within a
framework

Breathing new life into liturgy

TIM LOMAX

First published in 2001 by
KEVIN MAYHEW LTD
Buxhall, Stowmarket
Suffolk IP14 3BW

9 8 7 6 5 4 3 2 1 0

ISBN 1 84003 707 5
Catalogue No. 1500415

Cover design by Jonathan Stroulger
Edited and typeset by Elisabeth Bates

Printed in Great Britain

Contents

Foreword   7

Acknowledgements   8

About Tim Lomax   8

Introduction   9

Components that help bring worship to life   13

Good practice   23

Planning worship   33

Leading worship/services   37

Service outlines   41
  Third Sunday of Advent
  Third Sunday before Lent
  First Sunday of Lent
  Palm Sunday
  The Day of Pentecost
  Fourth Sunday after Trinity
  Seventeenth Sunday after Trinity
  A service exploring freedom in worship

Foreword

People's definitions of the word 'liturgy' are interesting. Some, seeing liturgy as a restrictive set of ancient words, believe liturgy quenches the Spirit and bores the people of God. Others, seeing liturgy as an imposition by the centre, believe it is good for doctrine but irrelevant to the local life of the church. And others, seeing it as a framework for freedom, rejoice in the way it can bring structure and opportunity for the worshipping life of the community of faith.

Common Worship ushers in a new chapter in the worshipping life of the Church of England. It contains ancient words (as well as modern). Its doctrine is agreed by the central bodies of the Church of England and as such is imposed on local congregations. But above all it is a set of structures and resources which will allow worshipping communities to express acts of praise which touch their local context and glorify God.

Tim Lomax has grasped this opportunity with both hands. In these pages you will find a creative imagination which takes the words and structures of *Common Worship* and does with them what was intended all along. Here music, action, silence – even smell and the visual arts – are all applied to make words come alive, and structures enable freedom. You may well disagree with the particular choice of a song or the application of an idea. But if you apply yourself to the principles behind the ideas, and give the planning of worship the time that Tim has, then you will be able to go beyond these ideas and find ways of worshipping which work where you are.

This book reminds us that God deserves nothing less than our best, and that we should never be satisfied (this side of heaven) in our expression of worship. For those of us for whom worship planning has often been last minute, these resources will come as an encouragement and a challenge. The Holy Spirit is not honoured by the slapdash, and is not there to make up for our lack of preparation. Perhaps the greatest tribute to Tim's work here would be for worship leaders to begin with his ideas, and then with prayer and creativity to plan acts of worship that are entirely different in their execution.

The Church of England has, for a while, put its worship at the centre of its agenda. This book takes the principles of *Common Worship* and applies them with style and imagination. May the churches of our nation do the same.

JEREMY FLETCHER
*Chaplain to the Bishop of Southwell and a
member of the Liturgical Commission*

Acknowledgements

A big thank you to Kate, John Darch, John Witcombe, John Leach, Mike Moynagh, Jonathan Bugden, Richard Lewis and Jeremy Fletcher for all their guidance, wisdom and encouragement. Thanks also to the many people who continually support me in my work, you know who you are!

About Tim Lomax . . .

His vision . . .

- To reflect the one who won his heart, to win the hearts of others.
- To present the gospel, strengthen discipleship and help lead genuine, accessible worship.
- To promote God's worth and word through music and song.
- To help build a twenty-first-century church.

Background . . .

Became a Christian at the age of 9. As a teenager, began to be involved in the music and worship of his local church. Studied music and teaching at the University of Derby before moving into full-time Christian work in 1995. Until 1999 he was music director/worship leader and Youth and Children's worker for his home church – St Andrew's and St Peter's, Weston Coyney, Stoke-on-Trent. Here, much experience was gained in planning and leading worship, mission work, all-age worship and the production of church services, not to mention multimedia youth events and schools work.

Now . . .

Tim and his wife Kate live in Nottingham. Kate is training for the ordained ministry at St John's Theological College. Tim now dedicates his time to music and worship under the name of his company – Lokate Music. He is also music co-ordinator for St John's College.

What does Tim do?

- Leads worship (solo or with the Lokate band).
- Composes worship songs.
- Creates contemporary forms of worship.
- Writes Bible-based liturgy.
- Provides worship workshops and training.
- Plans and leads all-age worship.
- Provides worship and music audits for forward-thinking churches.
- Provides teaching and lecturing on worship and music.

Web site: www.lokate-music.co.uk

Introduction

Using the Anglican *Common Worship* liturgies together with authorised material from *Patterns for Worship*, this book is designed as a user-friendly resource to help bring liturgy to life. A series of contemporary service plans are provided in a ready-to-use format. Within them spoken word, music, and creative ideas combine to provide a flowing journey of praise, response and openness to God. Use them together with the concepts and techniques of the opening chapters to develop worship, spark innovation or inject creativity.

Making dry bones live

So much of our worship of God is in words – we sing them, we speak them and we read them. In the Anglican Church we tend to use formal written liturgies to express our worship; beautiful prayers that give voice to our hearts using words we would struggle to find. However, on occasions within worship it appears that the only offering we give to God is printed words. There is a distinct lack of creativity or life. Rarely do we see imaginative ideas that enhance liturgy. So often there is little opportunity for personal expression or little expectancy for God to do a new thing. Sometimes we stifle the freedom needed for us to receive from God or express the wonderful gifts of the Spirit. Again we do little in response to hearing God's word. We forget sometimes that we *can* do more than say the Creed after a sermon. Words can often seem like dry bones in need of flesh around them. More is needed if liturgy is to come to life.

By setting liturgy in a creative and open framework we can bring worship to life and make dry bones live. We can stimulate more than the intellect by engaging the senses and the heart. Written liturgy is only the framework for worship and it should be regarded as scaffolding, not a cage. It provides a wonderful foundation to express heartfelt worship imaginatively.

The Church of England is privileged to have inherited the liturgies we use today. Surely it is our duty to use them to their full potential. It is of such benefit to have the basic framework provided through written liturgy. It helps us to worship in truth, focus our attention on God and structure essential elements of Christian living. Aspects such as forgiveness, prayer, belief, Communion and hearing the word of God are all given attention. However, there is the danger that we may hide behind liturgy and go through the motions. We can all too easily believe that the words have covered it all. To avoid this we must actively encourage individuals and churches to offer *themselves* within worship – their hearts, thoughts, gifts, experiences, desires, emotions, prayers and thanks. Such things are forever changing. God is Spirit and should be worshipped in a deeply personal way, from our spirit to God who is Spirit (John 4:24). We must also seek ways in which we can add life-giving components to liturgy. It is exciting to think that by including more than just the usual hymn slots, readings and sermon, worship can be transformed.

The following components can help bring liturgy to life:
- A desire to see the Holy Spirit impacting worship
- Praise

- Adoration
- Intimacy
- Reflection
- Silence
- Response to God's word
- Music and liturgy flowing together
- Open worship
- Extended times of sung worship
- Intercession
- Prayer ministry
- Freedom of expression
- Creativity

Note – Other components such as Holy Communion or Confession are essential to worship but are covered in detail within written liturgies.

The type of worship highlighted in this book aims to include the above components within a creative framework of written liturgy. Obviously, we have to guard against the 'recipe mentality' which plagues liturgy at the best of times. We presume that by including ingredients *x*, *y* and *z* the desired outcome will be realised. We should be mindful of this and remind ourselves that we are providing people with opportunities within worship. We are seeking ways in which we can encounter God and ways in which God can encounter us. Individuals and churches can be helped on their spiritual journey of growth by providing them with the opportunities to worship with all their heart. They will then depart from church changed, renewed, encouraged, healed or challenged and, God willing, filled with his Spirit.

Why use this book?

Perhaps you and your colleagues are wondering how to use the *Common Worship* material effectively and creatively. You may be thinking that you have lots of truth and not enough Spirit within your church worship. Maybe you would like to see more imaginative worship but lack the ideas, vision or time. Perhaps you have identified spiritual needs in your congregation that could be met through the introduction of this type of worship. Alternatively, you may wish to broaden your horizons and experiences as a leader of services or worship leader. This book has two parts; the opening chapters identifying the concepts and ideas to help bring liturgy to life plus a collection of eight ready-to-use plans and guidelines for innovative Anglican services (Communion and Services of the Word).

How do I use this book?

As a resource. It could act as a catalyst in the life of the church or in your own ministry. All the plans and ideas in this book are not set in stone, they are there to spark life. So, feel free to use them, adapt them and then invent your own!

Each service pattern provides a detailed plan suitable for principal (main) Sunday worship. Most are related to specific weeks in the lectionary year and can be used with the corresponding principal readings of all three *Common Worship* lectionary years. Most follow a theme (often related to Sundays in the church year). These can easily be adapted to fit particular readings of your choice, special events and times of change within your church. Each pattern is accompanied with full instructions to guide you and your colleagues through the worship. Song/hymn suggestions, worship components and other creative ideas can be followed, omitted or adapted to suit your own thoughts or style. These are all taken from *The Source*, *The Source 2*, *The Bridge* or *Release Songbook*, all of which are available from your local Christian bookshop or Kevin Mayhew Publishers. Further creative elements such as dance, drama or signing (as used for the deaf) can be added to each plan where appropriate.

Components that help bring worship to life

It is important to explain the components that can help bring liturgy to life. This will assist you in making better use of the service plans provided in this book. It will also help when introducing the components into your own service plans.

The components discussed below are applicable to all worship whether it is based around the *Book of Common Prayer* or the *Common Worship* liturgies. They can be incorporated into all types of services from regular Sunday services (Morning or Evening Prayer, Holy Communion and Service of the Word) through to Baptism, and Confirmation.

Incorporating such components will help facilitate worship that can be refreshed week after week, is creative both in planning and spontaneity and open to the work of the Holy Spirit.

A desire to see the Holy Spirit impacting worship

And with that he breathed on them and said, 'Receive the Holy Spirit . . .'
(John 20:22)

True worship expresses our relationship with God. We communicate our praise, adoration and prayers. We express belief, repentance and commitment. We respond to God's word. Written liturgy wonderfully encapsulates all of these things. Yet to leave it at this would mean that we miss out on the full picture and a complete relationship with God. As part of our life with him he has promised to be with us and in us by the power of his Holy Spirit. Through his Spirit he is ever present in our lives, our church and our services. This dimension of worship goes beyond words. God desires to make himself known and his presence felt. But without openness to the Holy Spirit and a desire to see him active (inspiring our understanding of the word, bringing personal growth and renewal, healing, empowering us with gifts of the Spirit) worship falls short of the wonderful kingdom experience God intends it to be. We can make Spirit-impacted worship our heart's desire and pray earnestly for God to move amongst us in power. Much of our worship already expresses this desire. The Eucharistic prayers, for example, acknowledge the presence of God's Spirit and our need of him. However, we can also express our desire for the Holy Spirit through other points within services. For example, **silence, reflection** or **extended times of sung worship** (*see also* **Open worship**, page 17).

Praise

Praise the Lord. How good it is to sing praises to our God, how pleasant and fitting to praise him! (Psalm 147:1)

When we gather together as congregations to praise Almighty God we join with all of heaven and earth. There is nothing greater than praising the Lord – as the psalmist says, it is good and fitting. When we truly know God we naturally desire to praise him (for his character, his love, his promises, his blessings, all that he has done and all that he is going to do). A praising church is an advancing people using praise as a powerful weapon in spiritual warfare, a growing people advancing in mission declaring praise inside and outside the church, and a rejoicing people who enjoy God. So then we should encourage each other in this pursuit and allow ourselves to express freely and gladly our heartfelt praise. Why not use **extended times of sung worship** to focus on praising God – for his character, for our Saviour Jesus Christ, for the blessings we enjoy or our thanks for all that he has done in our lives. Alternatively, use praise to conclude a service so that you leave having proclaimed God's might and victory.

Adoration

On coming to the house, they saw the child with his mother Mary, and they bowed down and worshipped him. Then they opened their treasures and presented him with gifts . . . (Matthew 2:11)

The underlying aim of all services is to worship God, to give him his worth ('worth-ship'). Adoration is defined as the act of worshipping. When we draw close to God and stay in his presence our desire is to adore him, expressing our intense admiration and offering our deep love for him. The Magi on seeing the Son of God in the form of a new-born baby bowed down and worshipped him. Today we now enjoy the opportunity to come into the house (the church building) and draw close to God through our *risen* Lord Jesus Christ. However, our response can be the same as that of the Magi. Within all services there should be the opportunity for us to bow down and worship our Lord. We need the space to open our own treasures and offer our gifts. Times of worship should enable us as Christians to declare our adoration of God and continually offer ourselves (all that we are and have) as living sacrifices. Again written liturgy provides an excellent framework for us to do this. We have access to words that express these sentiments wonderfully. However, we must allow people to express worship personally as well as corporately, spontaneously as the Magi did as well as with prepared words. We need to use liturgy effectively in order to lead people on a journey into the presence of their Saviour and provide them with space and time to dwell there. Sung worship and music can provide the environment for this to happen. We need to ensure that we use with sensitivity songs and hymns that express our adoration and combine them with written prayers imaginatively. Worship should flow naturally and we need to use liturgy to its full potential so that at an appropriate point we move from praise into adoration (*see also* **Extended times of sung worship**, page 17).

Intimacy

When a woman who had lived a sinful life in that town learned that Jesus was eating at the Pharisee's house, she brought an alabaster jar of perfume, and as she stood behind him at his feet weeping, she began to wet his feet with her tears. Then she wiped them with her hair, kissed them and poured perfume on them. (Luke 7:37-38)

Having drawn close enough to bow at the feet of the Lord and adore him we are now close enough to kiss him. In his presence we are aware not only of our sinfulness but also our forgiveness. Jesus has given us so much. His love for us is vast and we are overcome with gratitude and admiration. Our response – to love him unreservedly and to enjoy the intimate relationship he encourages. It is then that we are more aware of our feelings for him (love, gratitude, loyalty) and his closeness to us (his love in our hearts, understanding and warm regard). Just like the sinful woman we are at liberty to express our heart personally, freely, emotionally, despite what others think and regardless of cultural taboos. Similarly our worship becomes a fragrant offering to our Lord. Intimacy is an aspect of our relationship with God that we should openly encourage within services. Through it our relationship deepens and we grow in the love of Christ.

Intimacy is something that can be allowed for within the flow of any written liturgy. Teaching on this component of worship is invaluable and in this way you can encourage your congregation to seek it. **Extended times of sung worship** are effective in leading people to a point where they can enjoy it. There are many beautiful songs around which express aspects of our relationship with God. People can also rest in his presence whilst sensitive music is played at appropriate moments during or after songs.

Reflection

May the words of my mouth and the meditation of my heart be pleasing in your sight . . . (Psalm 19:14)

Have you ever left a church service feeling that you were never given the opportunity to catch your breath? You felt unable to respond to God on a personal level or give him what was in your heart at the time. Because you read the printed words and heard the minister speaking on behalf of the congregation you left feeling that you were spoken for. Maybe you were frustrated by not being allowed to express your faith or thoughts using your own words in your own way. I'm sure that many of us have encountered this. Unfortunately, it is rare to see space for personal or corporate reflection included within written liturgy. And yet it has such an important role to play in our spiritual lives. Worship should include time for us to think, meditate and ponder within God's presence. This can be done by introducing space for people to use how they wish; to think upon God's character or his love, to meditate on his word or as the hymn expresses so beautifully to 'ponder anew what the Almighty can do'. Why not try using sensitive background music after a time of sung worship or silence between readings and after the sermon. Alternatively, try to stimulate reflection by using drama, video clips, images, meditations or even songs to listen to.

Silence

But the Lord is in his holy temple; let all the earth be silent before him. (Habakkuk 2:20)

God makes his presence known to us within our place of worship. The simple response to his glory in our midst is reverent silence. Not because we show reverence by being silent but because when we truly know that we are in the presence of God we can be lost for words and want to remain still and quiet. However, silence before God is constantly neglected within our services. As a rule we tend to shy away from it, filling it as soon as possible. If only we could rediscover the value of silence we would have more to offer people who doubtless lead busy lives and crave to have their souls restored by quiet waters. Silence is such an easy component to include within worship whether it is planned or unplanned. Why not leave space for silence at appropriate moments after sung worship, during the prayer time or at the beginning/end of communion. By including silence you will also have the opportunity to encourage your congregation to listen to God and be open to receive gifts of the Spirit that can be expressed afterwards (e.g. prophecy, tongues).

Response to God's word

Do not merely listen to the word . . . (James 1:22)

God's word requires a response. We should be listeners and doers. This means that to conclude the Liturgy of the Word we can give space for a response process to start (e.g. commitment, repentance, healing or forgiveness). Perhaps an **extended time of sung worship** with response in mind, a period of quiet for people to begin reflecting on how they can act on the word, or a time of corporate prayer. The traditional Anglican response is the Creed. Although this is important it is only one form of response and we cannot expect it to fit every occasion and sermon. If God wants us to grow and give more of ourselves each time we worship we will not necessarily respond in the same way two weeks running! Why not introduce the Creed somewhere else within the service as in several of the worship plans contained in this book. This way worship benefits from an appropriate response and the Creed.

We can be imaginative when responding to God because we don't have to use words. Practical responses are a wonderful aid. They allow people to demonstrate what their heart is feeling. Usually they make use of simple ideas that allow people to visualise their response to God. For example, people can commit themselves to Christ by placing their thumb print on a large white cross. Whatever the method, it is vitally important that we do our utmost to introduce response within worship. By doing this the seeds of God's word are given the opportunity to be watered by the Spirit. Individuals and churches are free to start exploring what God's word means for them, to commit themselves to it and store it in their hearts as well as their minds. It is important, however, for the sermon to prompt a response. If a sermon is based on theory only, passing information on as in an academic lecture, then the word given will most probably prompt an intellectual response (or blank faces!). However, if the sermon challenges the heart too then it is more likely to prompt a heartfelt response.

Music and liturgy flowing together

By blending liturgy and sung worship as in the service plans provided, much of our worship can move in an unbroken flow. Instead of using isolated hymns or songs in between certain elements of liturgy, instrumental music (played by music group or organ) can link songs and provide a backdrop for the spoken word. At appropriate points the music can lead into the singing of hymns or songs. It is also possible to split a hymn or song with an element of liturgy.

For example:

Hymn: *Here Is Love* v1 → Intro to Confession, The Confession & Absolution → *Here Is Love* v2
[with background instrumental music   ]

(*See also* First Sunday of Lent service plan)

Linking songs/hymns with aspects of the liturgy will help bring the words of the service to life whilst adding meaning and relevance to the worship. Music can be a powerful tool. It can set the tone, create an atmosphere and spark emotions. Used with liturgy in this way it can help create an environment in which people are encouraged to offer heartfelt worship. Many churches use written liturgies that have been set to music. These can often provide beautiful and expressive ways of offering worship that moves naturally through liturgy. However, unlike spoken liturgy, liturgy set to music is not so easy to access. If people are to engage fully they need to be familiar with the melody of the music and this can only be achieved in time or through practice. This is worth consideration if you wish your church to be fully user-friendly for existing members and visitors.

Open worship

Times of **open worship** can be used simply to encourage openness to aspects of worship not included in a formal liturgy. Within them people can be free to express their praise or prayers spontaneously. Space may be given for testimonies and in some churches the sharing of spiritual gifts including prophecy, singing in the Spirit, speaking in tongues or words of knowledge. Specific opportunities can be provided for this as in the service plans included. Alternatively, people can simply be still and reflective if that is more in keeping with your type of worship. Worship leaders can help direct these times by encouraging an appropriate response or focus. Openness to the Holy Spirit should be prevalent. (*See also* **Freedom of expression**, page 19, for thoughts on further ways in which we can offer worship.)

Points to remember about open worship:

- To lead times of **open worship** you ought to be familiar and comfortable with them. You should expect the Holy Spirit to impact the worship!
- The congregation should also be encouraged to worship freely and be open to the Holy Spirit.

Extended times of sung worship

Instead of singing one song, a number of songs can be linked to form an **extended time of sung worship**. Put simply, worship is a journey. Times of sung worship can help us travel some of this journey. A collection of well-chosen hymns and songs can lead us through certain aspects of worship (see example below).

Example:

Praise → Adoration → Intimacy → Reflection/Stillness

In this example songs or hymns reflecting each of the above aspects could be linked within a time of sung worship. The congregation would be led naturally from one aspect to another until a point of reflection or stillness. Instrumental music could link the songs and provide additional space for personal reflection. Times of sung worship provide excellent opportunities for specific parts of services to flow and grow smoothly. The Church of England liturgies begin by calling us to worship and focus our attention on praising God. An **extended time of sung worship** would flow well from this. Alternatively sung worship could follow the sermon and lead people to a point of response. Worship of this type can also incorporate the idea of **music and liturgy flowing together** and **open worship** as outlined above.

Points to remember about **extended times of sung worship** –

- They can follow a worship flow or part of one (see section on Planning worship, page 33).
- The music should be led well and sensitively by the music group, worship band or organist (linking songs, providing beautiful background or instrumental music, worshipping through the playing of the music and touching people's hearts).

Intercession

Traditionally in services prayers are said by one person on behalf of others. However, if these prayers are to be truly 'of the people' we ought to include a little more freedom within the intercession liturgy. By doing this members of the congregation can offer their own prayers. Space provided in between sections of the prayers is an ideal way of engaging others either silently or out loud. We can also be creative with prayer and use more than spoken words. Subject headings on overhead or data projectors can prompt the prayers of the congregation, so too can newspaper headlines, photographs and video material. Background music either played live by the organ/ music group or recorded music can help create a prayerful atmosphere. By using simple ideas imaginatively intercession can more effectively encapsulate the prayers we wish to offer to God.

Prayer ministry

And pray in the Spirit on all occasions with all kinds of prayers and requests. (Ephesians 6:18)

In my view all main times of church worship should include opportunity for prayer ministry. It is one of the ways in which a church looks after the spiritual and physical welfare of its members. By making it available at appropriate times within the service people have the chance to ask for prayer and make their requests to God with the help of others. It also means that they can deal with issues highlighted during the worship. In addition churches can pray for those with specific ministries or those who are about to embark on them. When done effectively prayer ministry becomes an essential part of church family life. It is vital to note the value of training for this ministry and also the need to establish a framework for logistics (where will the prayer take place? when? will music continue? etc.).

Freedom of expression

Now the Lord is the Spirit, and where the Spirit of the Lord is, there is freedom. (2 Corinthians 3:17)

The Holy Spirit releases us in worship to express our hearts unreservedly. He enables us to worship with our whole being – body, mind and spirit. The Bible is littered with examples of how worship can be expressed. Therefore, in addition to the expressions of worship contained within written liturgy it is important that we actively encourage people to enjoy the freedom of expression that the Holy Spirit brings. This way they will have opportunity to worship fully and share gifts of the Spirit.

Space can be provided for *spontaneous expression* (aloud or private). This can be to speak prayers or truths about God, share testimony, proclaim victory, praise God, thank him or lament. Shouting is also a way in which we can express triumph, joy and victory (as with the Easter Acclamation). Opportunity for this type of expression can come at numerous points within a service. Probably the most natural would be within times of **open worship** or **extended times of sung worship**.

Expressing worship with our whole body is a good thing. Movement can capture emotion, enhance and even visualise our offering or response to God. *Dancing* is a wonderful form of physical expression. It is a sign of overflowing joy. Psalm 149:3 says 'Let them praise his name with dancing . . .' *Clapping* is something we are used to doing but not necessarily within worship. Just as we can applaud each other we can also applaud the Lord. Psalm 47:1 says 'Clap your hands, all you nations; shout to God with cries of joy.' *Raising hands* – 'Lift up your hands in the sanctuary and praise the Lord' (Psalm 134:2). The use of our hands can be a very expressive form of body language. To lift our hands in praise and prayer is a very clear indication of looking upwards and God-wards. *Bowing or kneeling* – 'Come, let us bow down in worship, let us kneel before the Lord our Maker; for he is our God . . .' (Psalm 95:6, 7). We humble ourselves in complete reverence 'for he is our God' almighty and awesome. These forms of expression can be encouraged throughout services. It must be stressed that they should not be done for tradition or for any other reason than to glorify God. They demonstrate how we feel towards him and if hearts are not engaged they are empty gestures.

The Holy Spirit also empowers Christians to express gifts of the Spirit. These include prophecy, speaking in tongues, interpretation, words of knowledge and healing. These gifts are given for the common good. Everyone does not receive the same gifts so this provides wonderful diversity and variety within the church. We should welcome gifts of the Spirit particularly within services, allowing them to shape and inspire our worship, church life and ministries. God makes himself known through his gifts and we should always be willing for him to do so. **Open worship** or **extended times of sung worship** can help provide the environment for spiritual gifts to be shared.

By providing biblical teaching and leading by example we can encourage congregations to be liberated in worship. It is our responsibility to provide worship environments that openly encourage freedom of expression.

Creativity

Creativity brings innovation and dynamism to worship. It can also bring relevance to each church in its local setting. It is something we ought to desire and facilitate in services as much as possible.

Singing new songs is something we should actively encourage. Not only is it biblical, it is also a great way to renew and refresh worship. Often new songs capture a moment in church life or spark new life. Keep a lookout for new music resources or sign up to a good publication series such as *Global Worship* from world wide worship (see address below) which provides the best of new song releases. You may well discover someone in your own church with a gift for songwriting. If this is the case then help them develop this gift by providing training or a mentor. It is important for good home-grown songs to be used and made more widely available. Perhaps include them in your worship and submit them (simple score and demo tape) to a publishing company. World wide worship are always on the lookout for new songs:

Praise & Worship Manager
world wide worship
Buxhall
Stowmarket
Suffolk
IP14 3BW

e-mail: www@kevinmayhewltd.com

When we are open to the creativity of the Holy Spirit within liturgy we may experience *music in the Spirit*. Obviously, the Spirit is present in all worship but sometimes he touches us very specifically causing us to respond spontaneously through music. Musicians can *play in the Spirit* creating improvised music and a beautiful environment in which we enjoy the presence of God – listening to him, perhaps speaking in tongues or just resting. At other times *singing in the Spirit* may spring from a time of sung worship. This is the spontaneous singing of a new song to the Lord. It may include the singing of tongues or more usual words of worship sung simply. It can come from an existing song and can move back into a song afterwards. It is not exclusive to musicians or worship leaders – it's for everyone. *Prophetic song* is something entirely different. It is a word from the Bible or direct from God which is sung by an individual instead of spoken. *Prayer song* can be spontaneous or pre-written. It is simply the singing of prayers. Some existing songs can act as a prayer of the people. At other times there can be sung responses to spoken prayers. Similarly to *singing in the Spirit, prayer song* can spring from a time of sung worship as people are inspired to sing out their prayers spontaneously.

One thing is clear, we need to be *imaginative* if worship is to be *creative*. Today through the media and modern technology we are bombarded with amazing sound- and sight bites. When a worship environment is built almost entirely on a collection of words (no matter how profound they are) it seems so lifeless in comparison to the stimulating experiences we receive in other places. This is not to say that we should merely seek an 'experience' through worship but that God has given us such stimulating tools to use creatively. By employing them we can form liturgy imaginatively.

To help increase creativity in worship you could use talented people from within your congregation. They don't necessarily have to be professional, just gifted, called and good enough to serve the church well. Don't worry if you don't have an array of creative people within your congregation. It doesn't mean that you are not open to creativity, just that you lack the people power.

Creative ideas to help stimulate the mind, heart and senses in worship

Music

- Combining liturgy with music.
  Music and spoken worship moving in an unbroken flow as in the worship plans provided. Musicians need to improvise sensitively and link songs with instrumental sections. Can provide a natural and beautiful worship environment.

- Background music to prayer, readings, meditations and reflections, visual elements, dance or mime. Requires improvised or recorded music to create the appropriate atmosphere.

- Songs to minister (live or recorded).
  Used at appropriate times within worship to encourage, convey a message, highlight a theme or lead to a point of response.

Visual elements

- Computer-generated images
- Art
- Video material
- Symbols
- Displays
- Banners
- Flags
- Stained-glass windows
- Icons
- Candles

Practical responses

- Visual and practical ways in which people can respond to God. For example, committing yourself to Christ by placing your thumbprint on a white cross (see First Sunday of Lent worship plan).

Animated liturgy

- Experiential liturgy that is *done* as opposed to *said*.

Examples:
Gathering, welcoming and fellowship could be made more of an experiential part of the opening liturgy. Songs or hymns reflecting a call to worship could be sung in the background whilst drinks and doughnuts are served.

For a service within Advent the worship could be conducted in darkness as much as possible. Towards the end of the service lights could be taken out onto the streets and the worship could be concluded there.

For a Passion Communion the room could be set out in the round with a low communion table placed in the centre of the circle. All could kneel around the table for The Peace and then remain there to share Communion with each other afterwards (see Palm Sunday worship plan).

Drama

- Sketches
- Mime
- Musicals
- Monologues
- Dramatised Bible readings

Meditation

- Looking at inspiring images, symbols or icons
- Imagination journeys or stories
- Written reflections

Movement

- Dance
- Signing (using sign language can not only help those who are deaf but also brings expression to worship)

Creative prayer

- Using images to inspire prayer
- Using video material to spark prayer
- Using newspaper cuttings (on OHP) to lead prayer
- Incorporating silence for personal prayer
- Incorporating space for prayers offered aloud
- Group prayer

Setting

- Seating
- Layout
- An environment of visual impact

Taste, touch and smell

- Incense
- Fragrant oils
- Meaningful objects to hold, e.g. scented petals, palm crosses
- Bread and wine
- Bitter herbs (from a Passover meal)

Good practice

All of us should strive to implement and maintain good practice within worship. Every church, regardless of size, wealth, resources and personnel, can work towards aims and goals within a structure of clear guidelines. Worship is the prime reason for a church's existence and those involved in the planning and leading of it need to know in which way they are headed and how to arrive there together. Good practice is a tremendous asset to any church. It can be the catalyst to spark effective ministry, it can create continuity within church life and, best of all, it can be passed on. Here are some aspects that help create good practice:

A vision that is shared

As part of every overall church vision there can be a specific vision for worship: how it will develop in the future, the spiritual needs to be met, the attributes it will contain, the beliefs it will be built on and how it will relate to the rest of church life. It is important that we do consider a vision for worship so that it is allowed to move and grow, incorporating the everyday things, new resources, effective ideas and, most importantly, what God is doing within each church. The vision, however, must be drawn up collectively and shared by the whole church. This may involve in-depth discussions, prayer and teaching.

Training

Training is vital to the implementation of good practice. It enables those involved in the planning, leading or supporting of worship to develop their gifts, skills and spirituality. If we are to enable church members to have effective ministries in the area of worship then we must be prepared where possible to provide them with appropriate training. We are not just talking about worship leaders, preachers or musicians. We must also equip others who play a part in services – those who lead the prayers, the prayer ministry team, drama team, dancers, signers, the welcome team, PA operators, etc. Why not find out what training is available from your diocese or seek out gifted people from your own congregation who may do in-house training. Alternatively, be on the lookout for conferences run by other churches or organisations.

Mentors

Providing mentors for those with ministries in the area of worship can be an invaluable strategy. Service and worship leaders, preachers, musicians and others with creative gifts can all benefit from trusted friends who guide, advise and teach from the wealth of experience they have gained. If mentors cannot be found within your own church try to find them from further afield.

Teamwork

This is a very biblical practice and can be put to very effective use within the area of worship. Often responsibilities in worship are shared but rarely co-ordinated. Each person does his or her thing in isolation from everything and everyone else. For example, often the person who chooses the songs and hymns does so without linking up with the people who will actually lead the service or preach. Now there is no doubt that God can still operate in such circumstances but it is certainly better to plan thoroughly, looking at the whole picture before focusing in on details such as songs. For this to happen teamwork is a must. One idea would be to create a worship-planning group responsible for the overall co-ordination. This would be made up of worship leaders, readers, music group leader/organist and group leaders for prayer ministry team, drama group, dance group, etc. They could meet to pray and discuss forthcoming services – responsibilities, content, themes, preachers, creative ideas and so on. All those involved would immediately have an impression of what will go on and would be able to prepare in advance. The worship leader for each service would then have co-ordinating and delegating responsibility for details such as service plan, songs/hymns, etc. This way all responsibility does not rest on one person (e.g. the vicar). By combining gifts worship benefits from collective planning.

Prayer

Prayer is an essential ingredient to worship and should be done in the planning and thinking stages, at any practices and before the actual service. Through prayer we communicate our need of God's inspiration and his Holy Spirit, our longing to see his will done and our desire to hear him speak to us. By praying at every turn from start to finish we give our gifts, ideas and plans to God for him to alter or confirm and then bless and use for his glory. Prayer for worship should involve all those concerned. Before services in the Church of England prayers are normally said in the vestry or chapel. For the most part these only involve the worship leader and preacher. Often other people involved in the service are not included. This is probably due to the fact that traditionally the leading of worship only involved a few people. Nowadays teams of people share the responsibility and should therefore share the responsibility for prayer.

Music

Music is one of the key elements to a service and can help or hinder worship. That is why its role is so crucial. Many clergy and church leaders have said that some of the most important church ministry appointments are the worship leaders, musical director and musicians. Music is a God-given part of worship. It can set the tone, help create a worshipful environment and give voice to our hearts. It is not sufficient to hold to the attitude that music simply accompanies singing and that all you need is any old set of accompanists. If someone can speak we don't automatically ask them to preach and so if someone can play an instrument this does not automatically mean they are suitable to help lead worship. There are other factors to consider – calling, gifting, heart and commitment. Obviously levels of ability vary from person to person and from church to church. However, if we take music as seriously as we should then we can work on a vision that encourages, trains and equips the dedicated people who play week after week. Often smaller churches struggle to find gifted musicians. This can cause some difficulties and often people who are unsure of their ability end up helping out. The important thing to remember is that all churches should develop the ministries of their musicians. If someone has the potential to improve and play music effectively within worship then it is the responsibility of church leaders to help him/her realise this potential. Some churches find that they have no one to provide music within services. Although this is not ideal it is not a disaster either. Unaccompanied singing or pre-recorded backing tracks such as *The Source* midi song files (available from DM Music www.dm-music.co.uk) can provide a suitable alternative to live instruments.

The music used in a service should make use of the best of the old and the new. It must also connect with the congregation with regard to age or social background, reflect the diversity of taste, be theologically sound (if in doubt leave it out) and be appropriate to the mode of accompaniment (i.e. piano, organ, band). New songs should also be introduced regularly (it's biblical!).

A great technique for song and hymn management is a play list. This is the complete list of hymns and songs appropriate for each church over a whole year. It can contain anything from 70 to 100 songs/hymns selected by a worship-planning group in consultation with the music group, organist, etc. The play list is reviewed every twelve months so that material no longer needed may be omitted and new material included. When the new songs and hymns have been chosen a new songs praise evening can be held. In time the songs on the list become very familiar enabling the congregation to participate confidently. A theme index can be drawn up for the list and OHP acetates can be made for all songs/hymns.

Obtaining copyright is a necessity if you are to reproduce any printed music or words to songs or hymns. The simplest way to do this is by purchasing a Christian Copyright Licence from

Christian Copyright Licensing (Europe) Ltd
Chantry House
22 Upperton Road
Eastbourne
East Sussex
BN21 1BF

Good resources are needed if church music is to be effective, drawing on the best of the old and the new. Ideally a church needs one good book to use as its basis for music (e.g. *The Source* – Kevin Mayhew). Then as new material becomes available (e.g. a series such as *Global Worship* – world wide worship) this can be added to existing resources. You don't have to buy duplicate copies of books either, just enough for all those concerned to have access to them (music group, vicar, other worship leaders). By purchasing a copyright licence you can then photocopy enough music for the musicians and singers. The photocopied music can be stored in files and used much more easily on music stands.

For the latest information regarding music resources visit:

www.kevinmayhewltd.com

Getting the best from the music group or worship band

This is something many churches struggle with. Often clergy and church leaders (who perhaps have little knowledge of music) are expected to establish a music group or oversee it. By including the following good practice guidelines more churches can hopefully be equipped with the knowledge they need to develop strong music groups.

The ideal make-up of the group

- Lead instrument (keyboard or guitar)
  To play the main part in the music.

- Lead singer
  To lead the congregation in singing the melody and call any instructions during a song.

- Support instrument (guitar or keyboard)
  To accompany the main instrument.

- Support/harmony singers (1 or 2)
  To accompany the lead singer with harmonies or to take over the tune at a given point in a song.

- Bass guitar
  To accompany the drum rhythm.

- Percussion
  To add sensitive rhythm.

- Acoustic instruments (1 or 2)
  To add extra harmonies or to play the tune for introductions, endings and instrumentals.

For contemporary services that incorporate **extended times of sung worship** and **open worship** the music leader (who is the lead singer and possibly plays the lead instrument) can be encouraged to become the worship leader. They will not necessarily lead the whole service and liturgy but certainly the aspects of worship involving music and singing. This is a role that many churches are developing and it must be stressed that it carries a lot of responsibility. The person who fulfils this role should be gifted, trained, appointed by the church and a team player. It is also important that they have a servant heart (as music is to serve not rule) and a clear sense of God's calling.

How should the group play together? – Simple is best

- With microphones you really only need one singer or instrument to pick out the melody at any one time.

- The group should be encouraged to improvise and be creative in their music. If they struggle encourage them to get some training.

- The group should be encouraged to play from chords given in a song. This will enable them to improvise more readily and become more musically versatile. Again seek training if required.

Qualities and attitudes to encourage within the group

- Worship, not performance; ensemble, not virtuoso solo.

- Everyone has equal status and is valued for their contribution.

- Servants of God and the church.

- The group should work hard to improve and set a high standard.

- Anyone involved in church music should have a clear calling and gift. They should be appointed by the church.

- Discipline is important. The group will need to be thorough, well rehearsed and prepared. Commitment, spiritual growth and maturity should be expected for such an important ministry.

Practices/rehearsals

- Should be times of worship and fellowship.

- There usually needs to be one main practice (approximately two hours if possible) plus warm-up and sound check before main worship (approximately 45 minutes where possible). Suggested outline:

  Drink and a chat
  Prayer
  Look at forthcoming service plans and requirements
  Immediate material (forthcoming week)
  Future material
  New material
  Prayer

- Plan worship thoroughly in consultation with the group and leader.

Position the music group well

This issue causes no end of problems in a church (within congregation and music group). However, there are several things to remember:

- The group should be seen (so that they can see the congregation and lead by example).

- The group should have sufficient space.

- Generally speaking the group need to be situated behind the PA speakers (to prevent feedback). You may need to reorder the church to find space. (This is a big issue but may be a real long-term advantage.)

Encourage the group

- The vicar or church leader should get to know the members of the group (socially and at practices). He/she can be their adviser and meet with them regularly – to discuss forthcoming services and events, plan, pray and discuss a vision for the music.

- The musicians should have the opportunity and freedom to express and develop their gifts.

- The group should be protected from unnecessary criticism.

- The group should be encouraged to grow as a team (fellowship, team spirit, etc.).

- Gifted group leaders or worship leaders should be encouraged to plan worship and select songs or hymns. They should also be a member of the PCC.

- Try to ensure that there is a good standard of sound equipment, operation and support available whenever the music group play.

Getting the best from the organist and choir

As organs and choirs are established aspects of many churches I'm sure most of you know how to get the best from them or to at least try. You will most probably have discovered that relationships are the key to either avoiding conflict or overcoming it!

Organist

- Meet with the organist and discuss what is expected of them.
- Choose appropriate material for the organist to play, i.e. hymns and songs that suit the organ. Otherwise frustration and blame may surface.
- If you have an organist and a music group then try not to make the organist feel second rate or out of date.
- Try to employ an organist from within the congregation or someone who is a Christian already. This is a spiritual ministry and must be treated as such. If you really must employ a non-Christian then make them feel part of the church and encourage them in their faith.
- Encourage wholesome attitudes:
    Servants of God and the church
    Accountable
    Worship, not performance
    Dedication
- Always discuss the choice of music, hymns and songs with the organist. Make your requirements and guidelines clear.
- If the organist is to select the hymns, etc., ensure that they know what to do and how to go about choosing appropriate material. Encourage them to seek training or advice if necessary.
- Give the organist sufficient warning of music needed so that they have enough time to practice.
- Encourage and enable the organist to develop their gift and ministry within the church.
- Support the organist and protect them from criticism.
- Encourage the organist to become a member of the PCC.

Choir

- Ensure the choir feel valued and appreciated.
- When undertaking major changes (e.g. reordering the church or introducing a music group) consult them and ensure that they feel part of the overall vision for worship in the church.
- The vicar or church leader should get to know the members of the choir (socially and at practices).
- Discuss vision, plans, services and expectations with the choir.
- Give members of the choir opportunity to develop in their faith.
- Encourage and enable them to express their gifts.
- Try to facilitate good relations between choir and organist and choir and congregation.

- Encourage the choir to grow as a team (fellowship, team spirit, etc.).
- Encourage wholesome attitudes:
    Servants of God and the church
    Accountable
    Worship, not performance
    Dedication
- Encourage the choir to pray together before practices and services.
- Keep them fully informed of requirements for services and the way in which music should be sung.
- Ensure that appropriate material is selected for the choir to sing.
- Support them and protect them from unnecessary criticism.
- Encourage them to use the best of the old and introduce appropriate new material.
- Encourage the leader of the choir to be a member of the PCC.

Combining a choir, organ and music group effectively

In many churches this can work well. Contemporary and traditional styles of music can be used together. The choir, organ and music group can each take responsibility for individual items within the worship (e.g. hymns = choir and organ, songs = music group). Alternatively, choir, organ and music group/band can combine for some of the music (e.g. a hymn played in a contemporary style – drum rhythm, choir singing harmonies and music group; organ joining for the final verse).

If you do use a choir and organ as well as a music group then it is important to build good relations. Help both groups to feel valued and needed. Set out clear guidelines as to what is expected of each. Involve them all in the drawing up of your church worship vision and show how each can help work towards it.

Additional creative elements

Although music is the main creative element of a service other elements (such as drama and signing) have an important role to play in some churches. The groups responsible for providing these must also be given attention. Many of the good practice points for music listed above can be applied to other groups. However, it is essential that planning and preparation for all creative elements is done as effectively, thoroughly and prayerfully as possible. This can be done drawing on the expertise of those people who are gifted at initiating such creativity within worship. All groups who offer ministries within worship need to establish themselves within the life of the church. For this to happen they ought to meet regularly to pray, practise and enjoy fellowship together.

Good PA system

To have good quality sound you need a good quality PA (public address system) and a trained PA operator. Understandably the budget is often the main concern. If you are in the fortunate position of obtaining good quality sound equipment there are a few points to remember:

- A good music group will require good PA resources.

- It's best not to amplify a music group through a PA system designed for spoken word, the sound produced will be poor quality.

- Small, less 'ugly' looking speakers are not necessarily the best.

- The acoustics of every church are different and so each has differing needs with regard to PA.

- Ask for professional advice to help you choose the best equipment for your church with the money you have available.

- When exploring the possibilities of installing a new PA system why not seize the chance to carry out any necessary reordering of space within the church.

Note – an organ and choir will require no amplification, so unless you have an additional music group a PA system for spoken word will suffice.

User-friendly worship

If worship is to be accessible to all, relevant and in touch, then it must be *user-friendly*. We should do our utmost to make people at ease with the liturgy we use. It should be simple to follow with printed words easy to find and read.

At the beginning of the twenty-first century we have so much opportunity to make liturgy ever more user-friendly. By employing the technology on offer printed liturgy or hymn and song words can be made readily accessible. We can use overhead projectors that make use of printed acetate sheets or in a few cases use video/data projectors that process computer-generated texts and images. Personal computer software also makes it possible to create professional standard service sheets for use within worship. Obviously this goes against the traditional book culture that dominates many churches. However, the experience of some churches has found that it is this culture that can help make church-going an off-putting experience. Newcomers and young people in particular are expected to wade through unfamiliar books often shifting from page to page or even from one book to another! This needn't be the case. There is so much potential for us to make church worship a user-friendly experience. All it takes is a little preparation and courage. The benefits are numerous. Firstly, you may find that you save money this way by spending less on projection or printed service sheets than you would on books. Secondly, you can be more creative and flexible by introducing alternative prayers, images and layouts appropriate to your particular church or community. Finally, the selection of hymns and songs becomes much freer when you are not tied to those included in the books you use. New songs can be introduced whenever you like (with proper copyright). Needless to say you may have to overcome some difficulties but don't lose heart. Innovative worship is not dependent on modern technology – it only helps. If you would like to see an increase in liturgy that is full of life then you will be able to achieve great things.

Here are some additional ideas that can help make worship user-friendly:

- Ensure that there is only ONE source for all words needed in a service (liturgy, hymns and songs). OHP or data projection are best but service sheets are also effective. (Note – data and overhead projection requires trained operators.)

- A trained welcome team on the door.
- A warm welcome at the start of worship.
- Clear guidelines to inform people of what goes on, where and how (concise).
- Refreshments before or after worship.
- No more than two new songs/hymns in a service.
- Strong, clear worship leading.
- Preaching that is full of life – including the everyday things, life application, stories, humour.
- Contemporary creative elements that link with everyday life.
- Space for people to offer themselves within worship (praise, adoration, thanks, prayers, needs, emotions, etc.)
- No jargon! If 'churchy' terms (e.g. 'imposition', 'archdeaconry', 'ecumenical') have to be used then explain their meaning.

Good resources

Good resources are vital to effective ministries. Be on the lookout for useful resources to equip any creative ministries you may have – music, drama, dance and signing. Also keep an eye out for new creative ideas to use – artwork, video material, images, icons, songs, etc.

Planning worship

The planning of worship is an important responsibility and should be undertaken thoroughly and prayerfully. Creative worship within a written liturgy framework requires detailed, careful planning. If worship is to flow, grow and create space for us to be open to God then we need to provide clear structure and guidance. We also need to be imaginative, open, collaborative and expectant in our approach. The following techniques will help you plan effective worship:

Making appropriate choices – factors to consider

- The type of service (Service of the Word, Communion)
- Time scale
- Who the service is for (all-age, adult)
- Composition of the congregation (social backgrounds, age)
- The setting (e.g. church layout)
- Church situation (renewal, building project, growth, conflict, struggling)
- Current prophecies or WOKs (Words of Knowledge)
- The theme
- The readings
- The liturgy to be used
- The desired worship flow (see **Choosing a worship flow**, below)
- Music needed:
  Background
  Instrumental
  Music to minister
- Where the music is needed
- Who is playing the music? (group, piano only, organ, choir)
- What creative ideas can be included? (artwork, drama, dance, responses, visual elements, etc.)
- Where should the creative ideas be placed in the service?
- The prayerful impression of what God might accomplish through the service

When considering the above factors it is important to discuss and prayerfully consider them with those taking part in the service (preacher, worship leader, organist, staff, etc.).

Choosing a worship flow

Worship needs a shape and it must flow so worshippers are led naturally on a journey. This way, aspects of worship will link well and follow on from each other smoothly. Written liturgy provides the framework for this flow but decisions still need to be made regarding how the worship will develop within the framework. A worship flow can be built from the following basic outline:

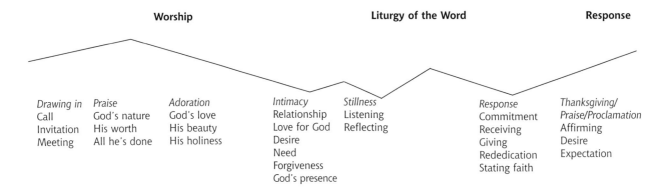

Worship	Liturgy of the Word	Response

Drawing in	*Praise*	*Adoration*	*Intimacy*	*Stillness*	*Response*	*Thanksgiving/*
Call	God's nature	God's love	Relationship	Listening	Commitment	*Praise/Proclamation*
Invitation	His worth	His beauty	Love for God	Reflecting	Receiving	Affirming
Meeting	All he's done	His holiness	Desire		Giving	Desire
			Need		Rededication	Expectation
			Forgiveness		Stating faith	
			God's presence			

Note – most of the service plans provided are also built on this basic worship flow.

When planning worship it is important to have an overall outline flow in mind. From that we have to decide what aspects will be included and the order in which they will flow within the liturgy framework. **Extended times of sung worship** can incorporate several of the aspects included in the flow. A safe principle would be to follow the above outline, but with good reason and well-chosen material, aspects could be omitted. Any decision would need to take into consideration the theme and other elements of liturgy that need incorporating. The desired worship flow is one that rises and falls naturally at appropriate places as in the example above.

Good examples:
Praise → Adoration → Intimacy → Stillness → Response → Thanksgiving

Drawing In →Praise → Stillness → Praise

Praise → Adoration → Intimacy → Response → Proclamation

The flow to avoid is one that is made up of alternate peaks and troughs.

Poor examples:
Intimacy → Praise → Drawing In → Response

Response → Praise → Thanksgiving → Stillness → Intimacy

Stillness → Praise → Intimacy → Thanksgiving → Adoration → Proclamation

Building worship on components that help bring liturgy to life

The following are the components discussed in 'Components that help bring worship to life', page 13. They can easily be built into any worship flow.

- A desire to see the Holy Spirit impacting worship

- Praise

- Adoration

- Intimacy

- Reflection

- Silence

- Response to God's word

- Music and liturgy flowing together

- Open worship

- Extended times of sung worship

- Intercession
- Prayer ministry
- Freedom of expression
- Creativity

Selecting hymns and songs

A simple principle applies; choose songs that fit with each aspect of your worship flow and liturgy. To make appropriate selections you will need to have an idea of the main characteristics for each song or hymn. You may find a theme index from a music book helpful.

Examples:
If you begin your service with praise then choose songs/hymns to fit this.

To conclude **extended times of sung worship** you may wish to bring people to a place of **intimacy**. Therefore choose a final song which reflects aspects of intimacy and relationship.

Later in the service you may include a time of **response** following the sermon. Choose songs appropriate to the response you wish people to make.

Points to remember . . .

- Choose hymns/songs that fit well together (these could then be linked by musicians).

- Avoid using songs at inappropriate places, e.g. songs of intimacy in times of praise or songs of repentance and cleansing after the confession and absolution.

- Many hymns/songs are versatile and can be used in a variety of places within a worship flow or liturgy because their words cover a lot of ground.

- Only choose songs/hymns that you have the words for.

- Try not to take a theme too literally (e.g. The theme is 'light', choosing songs with the word 'light' in the title).

- Always have a couple of songs up your sleeve just in case (for **extended times of sung worship**, **prayer ministry**, **open worship** or a song that flops).

- Use a good theme index (e.g. *The Source*).

Leading worship/services

Leading worship is not only a tremendous responsibility but it is also an immense privilege. The leader is not required simply to be the master of ceremonies but to be the facilitator of genuine worship that is full of truth and Spirit. As a service or worship leader you will have been called by God and appointed by the church. However, two further attributes are essential – a servant's heart and a willingness to be empowered by God. The following may help with your worship leading:

Worship is a journey

ensure that it flows and grows.

The importance of welcoming

Warmly welcome the congregation making visitors feel particularly welcome. Give clear guidelines regarding what will be going on and where things can be found, e.g. 'All the words you will need will be on the OHP'.

Demonstrating the value of praise and worship

If you do not process during the opening hymn or song then ensure that those leading worship or participating in some way are at the front of church when the sung worship begins. Otherwise a very clear message will be given out – 'this sung worship is an optional extra' or 'we don't want to be part of the proceedings just yet'.

How you treat hymns and songs also communicates a message. If you have to, try to introduce them well. Encourage all those helping lead the worship (e.g. the music group) to look as if they are enjoying themselves. It is essential that you and your colleagues lead by example.

Make the start and the end of a service clear.

After the opening sung worship avoid saying 'Our service/worship begins on page *x*' because it began minutes before with the singing of praise to God.

Introducing and directing (liturgy, readings, songs and hymns)

This is very important as it can make or break the flow of worship.

It is best if worship develops in an unbroken flow moving from item to item with very little announcing. For example, instead of announcing a hymn put the words on the OHP screen. As the music introduction begins people will quickly get the idea that they are about to sing. Similarly, with a reading. Why not let the reading follow another part of the worship unannounced so that one flows into the other? To do this, leaders of worship, musicians, those reading and praying will need to know what to do and when to do it (see the directions in the worship plans provided).

There may be times when announcing or introducing is necessary, e.g. when focusing a time of **response**, leading into an **extended time of sung worship** or directing how our worship may proceed. Whilst it is important to be clear it is also wise to keep it brief and simple.

Concluding sections of worship

Often it will be necessary to conclude what has already happened or to summarise parts of worship. Alternatively, you may feel you ought to conclude **open worship** or an **extended time of sung worship** with a prayer. Whatever happens, don't preach another sermon. Again keep it simple and brief.

Communication

It is important that during worship you are able to communicate with other leaders of the service (co-worship leaders, music group, preacher). This often happens during **open worship**, times of **response to God's word** or times of **prayer ministry**. The worship may need to go in a completely different direction and you need to ensure that it does. Inform your colleagues and always encourage them to advise you too.

Sensitivity

It is important that you have your eyes, ears and heart open to be aware of the Holy Spirit and things that God may want to do within worship.

If you feel prompted by the Holy Spirit to say something, challenge, encourage, prophesy or lead worship in a particular way then act on it.

Before the service pray you will be open to God and lead the worship with his guidance.

Open and willing

To allow God to move in power releasing our hearts in worship and opening our eyes to his will we have to be open and willing. If we want to be constantly in control then we will greatly limit any time of worship.

In short – go with the flow, don't be a control freak!

Facilitate

As a worship leader your role is to help facilitate genuine worship and the free moving of the Holy Spirit. Gentleness, humility and a desire for people to see God, not you, are essential qualities. If you want to be open to new dimensions in worship do it prayerfully with teaching and nurturing. Avoid imposing your own preferences and tastes.

Simplicity

Remember 'simple is best' – don't say too much. Often nothing needs to be said, the silence speaks for itself.

Be yourself, be human

Worship is not a performance and things will often go wrong. Have a sense of humour and remember that both you and the congregation are worshipping together, so enjoy it.

See for yourself

A lot of the ideas and techniques contained in this book may be new to you. In addition to introducing worship of this nature in your church why not experience similar worship for yourself. **Open worship** and **extended times of sung worship** are a main feature of celebrations at events such as Spring Harvest or New Wine. Alternatively, arrange a catalyst event or presentation to help develop the components that will help bring more life to the worship in your church.

For further information on 'bringing liturgy to life' worship events, training, church worship audits or conferences visit my web site: **www.lokate-music.co.uk**

Service outlines

Third Sunday of Advent – Service of Holy Communion
Theme: A witness to the Light

Order of Service

1   ***Welcome and Notices***

2   ***Introduction to the Theme***

Stand

3   ***Acclamation***

Restore us, Lord God of hosts:
show us the light of your face, turned towards us.

Will you not give us life again:
that your people may rejoice in you?

Show us your mercy, O Lord:
and grant us your salvation.

Blessed is the King who comes in the name of the Lord!
Peace in heaven and glory in the highest.

4   ***Sung Praise and Worship***

Hymn Lift up your hearts! (*Complete Anglican Hymns Old
and New*)
Song Great is the darkness (*The Source*)

5   ***Open Worship***

(Open to God, open prayer or praise, reflecting, sharing
gifts)

Sit if not already doing so.

6   ***Preparation and Confession***

Let us pray together:
Almighty God,
to whom all hearts are open,
all desires known,
and from whom no secrets are hidden:
cleanse the thoughts of our hearts
by the inspiration of your Holy Spirit,
that we may perfectly love you,
and worthily magnify your holy name;
through Christ our Lord. Amen.

When the Lord comes,
he will bring to light things now hidden in darkness,
and will disclose the purposes of the heart.
Therefore in the light of Christ let us confess our sins.

Directions

A small, unlit tea light candle should be
placed on every seat or pew, enough for all
who will attend. A large unlit candle
should be placed on a table visibly at the
front of church.

Warm and inviting. Visitors and newcomers
should be made particularly welcome.
SHORT PAUSE

Move directly into praise and worship

Play soft instrumental music in background.
Open to the Holy Spirit.
The congregation may be encouraged to
reflect, pray quietly or out loud. It is
important for the worship leader to direct
sensitively at this point.

Soft instrumental music continues in
background.

Most merciful God,
Father of our Lord Jesus Christ,
we confess that we have sinned
in thought, word and deed.
We have not loved you with our whole heart.
We have not loved our neighbours as ourselves.
In your mercy
forgive what we have been,
help us to amend what we are,
and direct what we shall be;
that we may do justly,
love mercy,
and walk humbly with you, our God.
Amen.

May the God of all healing and forgiveness
draw *us* to himself,
that *we* may behold the glory of his Son,
the Word made flesh,
and be cleansed from all *our* sins
through Jesus Christ our Lord. **Amen**.

Song Great is the darkness (chorus only)

Collect

O Lord Jesus Christ,
who at your first coming sent your messenger
to prepare your way before you:
grant that the ministers and stewards of your mysteries
may likewise so prepare and make ready your way
by turning the hearts of the disobedient
to the wisdom of the just,
that at your second coming to judge the world
we may be found an acceptable people in your sight;
for you are alive and reign with the Father
in the unity of the Holy Spirit,
one God, now and for ever.

7   *The Liturgy of the Word*

Reading 1
Short time of silence

Reading 2
Short time of silence

Sermon

Silence

Response – A call to be a witness to the light.

Song The Spirit of the Lord (sung during time of response)
    (*The Source 2*)

Towards the conclusion of the Absolution an extended introduction to the chorus of the song should be played.

Chorus should be sung more slowly and quietly to conclude time of Preparation and Confession.

SHORT PAUSE

Atmospheric music plays in background during the readings.
Photograph slide of 'Daybreak' or 'sprouting plant' projected onto screen.

After second reading member of congregation comes forward to light large candle.

(Photograph off. Candle remains lit.)

Sermon linked to theme. Challenging and affirming, giving practical help for discipleship.

For reflection on Sermon.
Background music plays softly during intro to Response and builds into the singing of the song. Lights are dimmed. Invite the congregation to answer the call to be a witness to the light – Jesus – to commit themselves to sharing the good news in word and action.

8 *Informal Peace* (optional)

Stand

9 *Affirmation of Faith*

Do you believe and trust in God the Father,
who made all things?
We believe and trust in him.

Do you believe and trust in his Son Jesus Christ,
who redeemed the world?
We believe and trust in him.

Do you believe and trust in his Holy Spirit,
who gives life to the people of God?
We believe and trust in him.

This is the faith of the Church.
This is our faith.
We believe and trust in one God,
Father, Son and Holy Spirit. Amen.

Instrumental music continues softly.

10 *Affirmation of Commitment*

Will you continue in the apostles' teaching and fellowship,
in the breaking of bread, and in the prayers?
With the help of God, I will.

Will you persevere in resisting evil, and, whenever you
fall into sin, repent and return to the Lord?
With the help of God, I will.

Will you proclaim by word and example the good
news of God in Christ?
With the help of God, I will.

Will you seek and serve Christ in all people, loving
your neighbour as yourself?
With the help of God, I will.

Will you acknowledge Christ's authority over human
society, by prayer for the world and its leaders, by
defending the weak, and by seeking peace and justice?
With the help of God, I will.

11 *Prayers*

Let us sit or kneel to pray together:
Come Lord.
Be our glorious King,
enthroned on the praises of your people.
Establish your Kingdom in the hearts of your church
and make us one in you.
Send us out in the power of your Spirit
to live for your praise and glory,
taking your light wherever we go.

Music ends.
Prayers continue unannounced.

Silence

We pray:
come, Lord Jesus.

Come, Lord.
Be our King of kings.
Before you all creation will sing your name,
every knee will bow and every tongue confess
that you are Lord.
May your Lordship be known through all the earth
and may your power be displayed.
We pray for our rulers and governments
and long that they too will acknowledge your authority
over every decision, issue and event.

Silence

We pray:
come, Lord Jesus.

Come, Lord.
Be our servant King.
Just as you sacrificed everything,
may we too give you our all.
Grant us your servant heart
so that we may give of ourselves freely.
Help us to love as you love us
and to reach out to those who do not know you.

Silence

We pray:
come, Lord Jesus.

Come Lord.
Be our victorious King.
You have defeated sin and death
and shown your power over sickness and suffering.
In faith we lift to you those who are suffering
through sickness, tragedy or bereavement.
Bring healing where there is none,
hope where there is despair
and life where there is death.

Silence

We pray:
come, Lord Jesus.

Come, Lord.
Be our one true King.
You have shown that there is only one path to walk,
one journey to make
and one direction in which to travel – towards you.
Help all Christian people who profess your gospel
to unite under your gracious power
and join with all the saints to cry . . .
come, Lord Jesus. Amen.

Stand

12   **(The Peace)** (If not shared already)

In the tender compassion of our God
the dawn from on high shall break upon us,
to shine on those who dwell in darkness
and the shadow of death,
and to guide our feet into the way of peace:
The peace of the Lord be always with you . . .
and also with you.
Let us offer one another a sign of peace.

All may exchange a sign of peace.

Offertory Hymn: O for a thousand tongues to sing
(*The Source*)

13   *The Eucharistic Prayer (E)*

The Lord is here.
His Spirit is with us.

Lift up your hearts.
We lift them to the Lord.

Let us give thanks to the Lord our God.
It is right to give thanks and praise.

It is indeed right and good
to give you thanks and praise,
almighty God and everlasting Father,
through Jesus Christ your Son.
For when he humbled himself
to come among us in human flesh,
he fulfilled the plan you formed
before the foundation of the world
to open for us the way of salvation.
Confident that your promise will be fulfilled,
we now watch for the day
when Christ our Lord will come again in glory.
And so we join our voices with angels and archangels
and with all the company of heaven
to proclaim your glory,
forever praising you and saying:

**Holy, holy, holy Lord
God of power and might,
heaven and earth are full of your glory.
Hosanna in the highest.**

We praise and bless you, loving Father,
through Jesus Christ, our Lord;
and as we obey his command,
send your Holy Spirit,
that broken bread and wine outpoured
may be for us the body and blood of your dear Son.

On the night before he died
he had supper with his friends
and, taking bread, he praised you.
He broke the bread, gave it to them and said:

After the Peace or prayers the hymn is announced.

Take, eat; this is my body which is given for you;
do this in remembrance of me.

When supper was ended he took the cup of wine.
Again he praised you, gave it to them and said:
Drink this, all of you;
this is my blood of the new covenant,
which is shed for you and for many
for the forgiveness of sins.
Do this, as often as you drink it, in remembrance of me.
So, Father, we remember all that Jesus did,
in him we plead with confidence his sacrifice
made once for all upon the cross.

Bringing before you the bread of life and cup of salvation,
we proclaim his death and resurrection
until he comes in glory.

Praise to you, Lord Jesus:
Dying you destroyed our death,
rising you restored our life;
Lord Jesus, come in glory.

Lord of all life,
help us to work together for that day
when your kingdom comes
and justice and mercy will be seen in all the earth.

On the words 'come in glory' instrumental introduction to 'Great is the darkness' begins.

Look with favour on your people,
gather us in your loving arms
and bring us with *(N and)* all the saints
to feast at your table in heaven.

Through Christ, and with Christ, and in Christ,
in the unity of the Holy Spirit,
all honour and glory are yours, O loving Father,
for ever and ever.
Amen.

Song Great is the darkness (chorus only)

Sing softly to conclude Eucharistic Prayer.

14   *The Lord's Prayer*

Music ends.

Let us sit or kneel as we pray for the coming of God's
kingdom in the words our Saviour taught us:

Our Father in heaven,
hallowed be your name,
your kingdom come,
your will be done,
on earth as in heaven.
Give us today our daily bread.
Forgive us our sins
as we forgive those who sin against us.
Lead us not into temptation
but deliver us from evil.
For the kingdom, the power,
and the glory are yours
now and for ever. Amen.

15 *Breaking of the Bread*

The president breaks the consecrated bread.
Every time we eat this bread and drink this cup:
We proclaim the Lord's death until he comes.

Giving of Communion

Draw near with faith.
Receive the body of our Lord Jesus Christ
which he gave for you,
and his blood which he shed for you.
Eat and drink in remembrance that he died for you,
and feed on him in your hearts
by faith with thanksgiving.

The president and people receive communion.
Authorised words of distribution are used.

Songs How deep the Father's love for us (*The Source*)
Such love (*The Source*)
Thank you for saving me (*The Source*)

16 *Prayer after Communion*

We give you thanks, O Lord, for these heavenly gifts;
kindle in us the fire of your Spirit
that when your Christ comes again
we may shine as lights before his face;
who is alive and reigns now and for ever. **Amen.**

Almighty God,
we thank you for feeding us
with the body and blood
of your Son Jesus Christ.
Through him we offer you
our souls and bodies
to be a living sacrifice.
Send us out in the power of your Spirit
to live and work to your praise and glory. Amen.

Stand

Song We'll walk the land (*The Source*) or
Men of faith (*The Source*)

All move outside on to the street for the conclusion of the
worship. Torches, lanterns or candles are taken if done at night.

17 *The Blessing and Dismissal*

Christ the Sun of Righteousness shine upon you,
scatter the darkness from before your path,
and make you ready to meet with him
when he comes in glory;
and the blessing of God almighty,
the Father, the Son and the Holy Spirit,
be among you and remain with you always.

Go in peace to love and serve the Lord.
In the name of Christ. Amen.

Intro to the song begins immediately after the prayer.

Third Sunday before Lent – Service of Holy Communion
Theme: God's gift of grace

Order of Service

Grace, mercy and peace
from God our Father
and the Lord Jesus Christ
be with you
and also with you.

1 **Welcome and Notices**

2 **Introduction to the Theme**

Stand

Song Praise the Lord (*The Source 2*) or
Let everything that has breath (*The Bridge*)

3 **Preparation and Confession**

Let us sit or kneel as we pray together:
**Almighty God,
to whom all hearts are open,
all desires known,
and from whom no secrets are hidden:
cleanse the thoughts of our hearts
by the inspiration of your Holy Spirit,
that we may perfectly love you
and worthily magnify your holy name;
through Christ our Lord. Amen.**

God so loved the world
that he gave his only Son Jesus Christ
to save us from our sins,
to be our advocate in heaven,
and to bring us to eternal life.

Let us confess our sins in penitence and faith,
firmly resolved to keep God's commandments
and to live in love and peace with all.

**Almighty God, our heavenly Father,
we have sinned against you
and against our neighbour
in thought and word and deed,
through negligence, through weakness,
through our own deliberate fault.
We are truly sorry
and repent of all our sins.**

Directions

Warm and inviting. Visitors and newcomers
should be made particularly welcome.

SHORT PAUSE

After the song has been sung all the way
through slow the music down and repeat
the chorus slowly a couple of times.

Softer instrumental music then continues in
the background.

For the sake of your Son Jesus Christ,
who died for us,
forgive us all that is past
and grant that we may serve you in newness of life
to the glory of your name.
Amen.

Almighty God,
who forgives all who truly repent,
have mercy upon *you*,
pardon and deliver *you* from all *your* sins,
confirm and strengthen *you* in all goodness,
and keep *you* in life eternal;
through Jesus Christ our Lord.
Amen.

Stand

Songs: Thank you for the blood (*WWW 2*)
          Greater grace (*The Source 2*)

4 ***Open Worship***

(Open to God, open prayer or praise, reflecting, sharing gifts)

5 ***Silence***

Collect

Almighty God,
who alone can bring order
to the unruly wills and passions of sinful humanity:
give your people grace
so to love what you command
and to desire what you promise,
that, among the many changes of this world,
our hearts may surely there be fixed
where true joys are to be found;
through Jesus Christ your Son our Lord,
who is alive and reigns with you,
in the unity of the Holy Spirit,
one God, now and for ever. Amen.

Sit if not already doing so.

6 ***The Liturgy of the Word***

Reading 1
Short time of silence

Reading 2
Short time of silence

Sermon

7 ***Silence***

During the Absolution the music moves smoothly into the introduction to the next song and builds in volume.

Instrumental music continues gently in the background during Open Worship. Worship leader must be sensitive, lead clearly and go with the flow of worship.

Music ends.

SHORT PAUSE

For personal reflection and response to Sermon. How does God want me to respond? Maybe guide people's prayers as an opportunity for response.

8 *Extended Time of Sung Worship*

Stand initially but people should be free to stand or sit

Songs Thank you for the blood (Reprise)

There's a place where the streets shine (*The Source*)

O Lord, you're beautiful (*The Source*)

Songs linked together with instrumental music.

9 *Open Worship*

(Open to God, open praise, reflecting, sharing gifts)

Gentle music continues in the background.

10 *Open Prayer*

Sit or kneel if not doing so already.

As music continues very softly members of the congregation are encouraged to speak out their prayers or to pray privately. Reassure people that they are not under pressure to pray aloud. Prayer headings could be shown on the OHP as a guide.

Merciful Father,
accept these prayers
for the sake of your Son,
our Saviour Jesus Christ.
Amen.

The music ends.

The Creed

Let us stand to say the Creed:

We believe in one God,
the Father, the Almighty,
maker of heaven and earth,
of all that is,
seen and unseen.

We believe in one Lord, Jesus Christ,
the only Son of God,
eternally begotten of the Father,
God from God, Light from Light
true God from true God,
begotten, not made,
of one Being with the Father;
through him all things were made.
For us and for our salvation
he came down from heaven,
was incarnate from the Holy Spirit
and the Virgin Mary,
and was made man.
For our sake he was crucified under Pontius Pilate;
he suffered death and was buried.
On the third day he rose again
in accordance with the Scriptures;
he ascended into heaven
and is seated at the right hand of the Father.
He will come again in glory
to judge the living and the dead,
and his kingdom will have no end.

We believe in the Holy Spirit,
the Lord, the giver of life,
who proceeds from the Father and the Son,
who with the Father and the Son
is worshipped and glorified,
who has spoken through the prophets.

**We believe in one holy, catholic and apostolic Church.
We acknowledge one baptism
for the forgiveness of sins.
We look for the resurrection of the dead,
and the life of the world to come. Amen.**

11 *The Liturgy of the Sacrament*

The Peace

God is love
and those who live in love live in God
and God lives in them.

The peace of the Lord be always with you
and also with you.

Let us offer one another a sign of peace.

All may exchange a sign of peace.

12 *The Gifts of the People and the Gifts for the People*

(The collection plate is passed around and also a basket
or plate containing chocolates or sweets. People are
invited to give and receive.)

Song To listen to and to minister (live or recorded)
Wonderful grace (Global Worship – *Wonderful Grace*
CD or *Source 2*)

Played during the time of giving.

Music ends.

Yours, Lord, is the greatness, the power,
the glory, the splendour, and the majesty;
for everything in heaven and on earth is yours.
**All things come from you,
and of your own do we give you.**

13 *The Eucharistic Prayer (H)*

Remain seated.

The Lord be with you
and also with you.

Lift up your hearts.
We lift them to the Lord.

Let us give thanks to the Lord our God.
It is right to give thanks and praise.

It is right to praise you, Father, Lord of all creation;
in your love you made us for yourself.

When we turned away
you did not reject us,
but came to meet us in your Son.
**You embraced us as your children
and welcomed us to sit and eat with you.**

In Christ you shared our life
that we might live in him and he in us.
**He opened his arms of love upon the cross
and made for all the perfect sacrifice for sin.**

On the night he was betrayed,
at supper with his friends
he took bread, and gave you thanks;
he broke it and gave it to them, saying:
Take, eat; this is my body which is given for you;
do this in remembrance of me.
Father, we do this in remembrance of him:
his body is the bread of life.

At the end of supper, taking the cup of wine,
he gave you thanks, and said:
Drink this, all of you;
this is my blood of the new covenant,
which is shed for you for the forgiveness of sins;
do this in remembrance of me.
Father, we do this in remembrance of him:
his blood is shed for all.

As we proclaim his death
and celebrate his rising in glory,
send your Holy Spirit that this bread and this wine
may be to us the body and blood of your dear Son.

As we eat and drink these holy gifts
make us one in Christ, our risen Lord.

With your whole Church throughout the world
we offer you this sacrifice of praise
and lift our voice to join the eternal song of heaven:

Holy, holy, holy Lord,
God of power and might,
heaven and earth are full of your glory.
Hosanna in the highest.

14 *The Lord's Prayer*

Let us pray for the coming of God's kingdom in the
words our Saviour taught us:
Our Father in heaven,
hallowed be your name,
your kingdom come,
your will be done,
on earth as in heaven.
Give us today our daily bread.
Forgive us our sins
as we forgive those who sin against us.
Lead us not into temptation
but deliver us from evil.
For the kingdom, the power,
and the glory are yours
now and for ever. Amen.

Breaking of the Bread

15

The president breaks the consecrated bread.
We break this bread to share in the body of Christ.
Though we are many, we are one body, because we
all share in one bread.

16 *Giving of Communion*

Draw near with faith.
Receive the body of our Lord Jesus Christ
which he gave for you,
and his blood which he shed for you.
Eat and drink
in remembrance that he died for you,
and feed on him in your hearts
by faith with thanksgiving.

Songs By his grace (*The Source*)
Here is love (*The Source*)
Thank you for saving me (*The Source*)

Songs are linked through instrumental music.

17 *Silence*

18 *Prayer after Communion*

Merciful Father,
who gave Jesus Christ to be for us the bread of life,
that those who come to him should never hunger:
draw us to the Lord in faith and love,
that we may eat and drink with him
at his table in the kingdom,
where he is alive and reigns, now and for ever.

Father of all,
we give you thanks and praise,
that when we were still far off
you met us in your Son and brought us home.
Dying and living, he declared your love,
gave us grace, and opened the gate of glory.
May we who share Christ's body live his risen life;
we who drink his cup bring life to others;
we whom the Spirit lights give light to the world.
Keep us firm in the hope you have set before us,
so we and all your children shall be free,
and the whole earth live to praise your name;
through Christ our Lord.
Amen.

Music introduction to the approaching song begins softly and builds during the prayer.

Song I could sing unending songs (*The Source*)

After the Amen the music introduction leads strongly into the song.

Before the Blessing and Dismissal offer prayer ministry for those in need of it. Maybe someone wants healing or perhaps something has been highlighted during the worship and they would like prayer for that.

19 *The Blessing and Dismissal*

The peace of God,
which passes all understanding,
keep your hearts and minds
in the knowledge and love of God,
and of his Son Jesus Christ our Lord;
and the blessing of God almighty,
the Father, the Son and the Holy Spirit,
be among you and remain with you always. **Amen.**

Go in peace to love and serve the Lord.
In the name of Christ. Amen.

20 **The Grace** (sung) (*The Source 2*)

> **The grace of our Lord Jesus Christ**
> **and the love of God**
> **and the fellowship of the Holy Spirit**
> **be with us for evermore.**

21 *Prayer Ministry Available*

Soft worship music could be played as people leave or as prayer continues.

First Sunday of Lent – Service of the Word
Theme: Repent, believe and follow

Order of Service

1 Welcome and Notices

2 Introduction to the Theme

Stand

3 Sentence of Scripture and Acclamation

'The kingdom of God is near.
Repent and believe the good news!' (Mark 1:15)

Let us give thanks to the God of our Lord Jesus Christ:
who has blessed us in Christ with every spiritual blessing.

Before the world was made, God chose us in Christ:
that we might be holy and blameless before him.

Let us praise God for the glory of his grace:
for the free gift he gave us in his dear Son.

To Father, Son and Holy Spirit:
give praise and dominion, honour and might, for ever and ever. Amen.

4 Extended Time of Sung Worship

Hymn To God be the glory (*The Source*) or
Song Salvation belongs to our God (*The Source*)
Song There is a Redeemer (*The Source*) or
Song I will offer up my life (*The Source*)

5 Silence (except for music)

6 Open Worship

(Open to God, open prayer or praise, reflecting, sharing gifts)

Sit if not already doing so.

7 Psalm (see Lectionary)

8 Confession

Hymn Here is love (verse 1) (*The Source*)

Let us admit to God the sin which always confronts us.
**Lord God, we have sinned against you;
we have done evil in your sight.
We are sorry and repent.**

Directions

Stand a large white cross (card or paper-covered wood) clearly at front of church.

Warm and inviting. Visitors and newcomers should be made particularly welcome.

SHORT PAUSE

Read sentence without announcing it. With feeling and enthusiasm.

Move directly into acclamation.

Introduction to first hymn begins immediately after Acclamation.

Hymn and songs linked through instrumental music.

Soft instrumental music continues.

The congregation may be encouraged to pray out loud, speak out praise or to share how God has encouraged them.
Worship leader may conclude with an appropriate prayer.

Read together if possible.

Soft introduction to hymn.

Soft instrumental music continues in background to prayer.

Have mercy on us according to your love.
Wash away our wrongdoing
and cleanse us from our sin.
Renew a right spirit within us
and restore us to the joy of your salvation,
through Jesus Christ our Lord. Amen.

May the Father of all mercies,
cleanse *us* from *our* sins,
And restore *us* in his service
to the praise and glory of his name,
through Jesus Christ our Lord. **Amen.**

Hymn Here is love (verse 2) (*The Source*)

> Instrumental leads into intro to verse 2 of hymn.

Collect
Almighty God,
whose Son Jesus Christ fasted forty days
in the wilderness,
and was tempted as we are, yet without sin:
give us grace to discipline ourselves
in obedience to your Spirit;
and, as you know our weakness,
so may we know your power to save;
through Jesus Christ your Son, our Lord,
who is alive and reigns with you,
in the unity of the Holy Spirit,
one God, now and for ever.

> Music ends.

9   *The Liturgy of the Word*

Reading 1
Short time of silence

Reading 2
Short time of silence

> Photograph slide of 'footprints in sand' or 'a child's hand held in Father's hand' projected onto the screen during the readings. No announcement of the readings. Should be unbroken time of listening and reflecting.

Sermon

> Sermon linked to theme. Challenging and affirming, giving practical help for discipleship.

10   *Silence*

> For reflection on Sermon.

11   *Response*

> Background music plays softly during introduction to Response.
> As it is the start of Lent, invite the congregation to follow Christ. Perhaps for the first time or in a deeper way. Turning away from old ways or sins, believing with a sincere heart in his forgiveness and all that he offers.

Personal rededication through private prayer,

or

A practical dedication by placing your own ink thumb-print on the white cross at the front of church.

> Music continues whilst people respond to Christ privately.
>
> If members of congregation wish to dedicate themselves to Christ then invite them to respond practically by pledging themselves to the cross of Christ, placing their thumb-print on the white cross at the front of church. This would be their own unique pledge as no one else shares their thumb-print identity. Music moves into song of worship to sing during Response.

Song From heaven you came (*The Source*)

The free gift of God is eternal life in Christ Jesus our Lord.
By his mercy we present our whole lives to God as a living sacrifice.

12 *Prayers*

Let us sit or kneel to pray:

Lord, we want to follow you in the way of a servant.
Give us the strength to let go of our selfish desires
as individuals and as a church,
to deny ourselves for the sake of others.
Help us to make it our priority to serve you
by sharing your love in all that we do and say.

Silence

Lord, we'll follow you.
Help us to walk in your footsteps.

Lord, we want to follow you in the way of sacrifice.
May your death on the cross remind us
of all that you gave to bring us forgiveness
and help us to count the cost of truly following you.

Silence

Lord, we'll follow you.
Help us to walk in your footsteps.

Lord, we want to follow you in the way of peace.
We ask that you would give all people the strength
to resist war and hate, to forgive and live in love.
Through your Spirit help your church to shine
an example of your love and to embrace the lost,
the despised and those rejected.

Silence

Lord, we'll follow you.
Help us to walk in your footsteps.

Lord, we want to follow you in the way of compassion.
Help us to love as you love us.
May we help you in the work of your kingdom
by bringing comfort to the sick and suffering.
We pray now for those who are suffering at this time
and ask that you will give them the healing touch
of your precious hands.

Silence

Show us how we might help them in practical ways,
giving them friendship and support.

Lord, we'll follow you.
Help us to walk in your footsteps.

Lord, we want to follow you to the gates of glory.
You have walked the path from death into glorious life
and now you lead the way to the place
where we can live with you for ever,
joining with all the saints in your endless praise.

Conclude with this statement of dedication.

SHORT PAUSE

Move directly into prayers without announcing.

Lord we'll follow you.
Help us to walk in your footsteps. Amen.

Offertory Hymn Breathe on me, Breath of God
(*The Source*)

Remain standing

13   *Final Prayers*

**God of our pilgrimage,
you have led us to the living water.
Refresh and sustain us
as we go forward on our journey,
in the name of Jesus Christ our Lord. Amen.**

The Lord God Almighty is our Father:
he loves us and tenderly cares for us.

The Lord Jesus Christ is our Saviour:
he has redeemed us and will defend us to the end.

The Lord, the Holy Spirit, is among us:
**he will lead us in God's holy way.
To God Almighty, Father, Son and Holy Spirit,
be praise and glory today and for ever. Amen.**

Song Before the throne of God above (*The Source 2*)

14   *The Grace* (sung) (*The Source 2*)

**The grace of our Lord Jesus Christ
and the love of God
and the fellowship of the Holy Spirit
be with us for evermore.**

15   *Prayer Ministry Available*

Announce hymn whilst music introduction is played in background.

Before the final songs offer the opportunity for prayer after the service. Maybe people would like to make their pledge on the cross as they felt unable to respond in front of the whole congregation. Perhaps the worship highlighted a need for prayer or advice.

Soft music could be played as people leave and whilst prayer continues.

Palm Sunday – Service of Holy Communion
Liturgy of the Passion

Preparation

This worship could be simple and without trimmings.
It would be most fitting for this service to be conducted in the round where possible. The altar or Communion table would be situated in the centre of the congregation and the worship should be led and directed also from within the circle. A table low to the floor could be used for Communion and the congregation could also sit on the floor instead of chairs. Cushions could be used and some chairs placed around the outer circle for those who need them. For the Eucharist the president could kneel. At the distribution members of the congregation could kneel around the table and informally offer one another the bread and wine. Instead of silverware, pottery cups and plates could be used. An unleavened loaf and red wine should make up the meal. For visual inspiration, a bowl or basin and towel could be placed next to the Communion table. For easy access to the words of the worship it would be best to use a service sheet. Sung worship and music should be simple and sensitive. Perhaps unaccompanied singing or simple harmony would be appropriate.

Order of Service

Directions

1 Welcome and Notices

Warm and inviting. Visitors and newcomers should be made particularly welcome.

2 Introduction to the Service and Theme

Grace, mercy and peace
from God our Father
and the Lord Jesus Christ
be with you
and also with you.

SHORT PAUSE

3 Extended Time of Sung Worship

Stand

Songs We bow down (*The Source 2*)
I bow my knee before your throne (*The Source*)
Every knee shall bow (*The Bridge*)

Move directly into sung worship.

Songs may be linked together with instrumental music.

4 Open Worship

(Open to God, open prayer or praise, reflecting, sharing gifts)

The congregation may be encouraged to reflect, express gifts of the Spirit or pray out loud. It is important for the worship leader to direct sensitively at this point.

5 Silence

6 Preparation and Confession

Let us sit or kneel as we pray together:

Almighty God,
to whom all hearts are open,
all desires known,
and from whom no secrets are hidden:
cleanse the thoughts of our hearts
by the inspiration of your Holy Spirit,
that we may perfectly love you,
and worthily magnify your holy name;
through Christ our Lord. Amen.

God shows his love for us
in that, while we were still sinners, Christ died for us.
Let us then show our love for him
by confessing our sins in penitence and faith.

We pray together:
**Most merciful God,
Father of our Lord Jesus Christ,
we confess that we have sinned
in thought, word and deed.
We have not loved you with our whole heart.
We have not loved our neighbours as ourselves.
In your mercy
forgive what we have been,
help us to amend what we are,
and direct what we shall be;
that we may do justly,
love mercy,
and walk humbly with you, our God.
Amen.**

Almighty God,
who forgives all who truly repent,
have mercy upon *you*,
pardon and deliver *you* from all *your* sins,
confirm and strengthen *you* in all goodness,
and keep *you* in life eternal;
through Jesus Christ our Lord.
Amen.

Collect

Almighty and everlasting God,
who in your tender love towards the human race
sent your Son our Saviour Jesus Christ
to take upon him our flesh
and to suffer death upon the cross:
grant that we may follow the example
of his patience and humility,
and also be made partakers of his resurrection;
through Jesus Christ your Son our Lord,
who is alive and reigns with you,
in the unity of the Holy Spirit,
one God, now and for ever. **Amen.**

7   *The Liturgy of the Word*

Reading
Short time of silence

No announcement of the readings. Should be an unbroken time of listening and reflecting.

Gospel Reading
Short time of silence

Sermon

Sermon linked to theme and readings. Informative but also challenging and affirming. Should lead people to point of response or action encouraging them on their journey of discipleship.

8   *Silence*

For reflection and prayerful response

Worship leader should initiate and guide people's response during silence.

9 *Prayers*

The prayers follow the silence unannounced.

If we have any encouragement
from being united with Christ,
if any comfort from his love,
if any fellowship from the Spirit,
if any tenderness or compassion,
then let us be like minded, having the same love,
being one in Spirit and purpose.
Let us do nothing out of selfish ambition or vain conceit,
but in humility consider others better than ourselves.
Each of us should look not only to our own interests,
but also to the interests of others.
Our attitude should be the same as that of Christ Jesus.
Grant us, Lord, **your servant heart. Amen.**

Lord, you are in very nature God.
You made yourself nothing
and took the very nature of a servant,
being made in human likeness.
You humbled yourself and became obedient to death
– even death on a cross!
Help all our leaders in government and in the church
to reflect in some small way
the same humility and self-denial.
By putting the lives of others first
and sacrificing their own interests
they will lead by the best of examples
and reflect you, the servant king
who made humility a way of life.

Silence

Grant us, Lord, **your servant heart. Amen.**

Master, God exalted you to the highest place
and gave you the name that is above every name.
That at the name of Jesus every knee should bow,
in heaven and on earth and under the earth,
and every tongue confess that you are Lord,
to the glory of God the Father.

We pray that your name will be exalted
in all the earth,
that the people of this nation will know you are Lord,
that this church will be a place
where people meet with you,
and that we will make you visible wherever we go.

Silence

Jesus, as Lord of all we ask you to be near to those in
need – the sick, the grieving, the lonely and the poor.

Silence

Lord you have the power to heal and to save
and we ask you to bring healing and wholeness
where there is pain and suffering.
We ask too that you will empower us with your Spirit
and send us out to serve people with your love.

Grant us, Lord, **your servant heart. Amen.**

PAUSE

O God, help us to carry on working out our salvation
with fear and trembling,
for it is you who works in us
to will and to act according to your good purpose.
May we shine like stars in the heavens
as we hold out the word of life
and each day join with all the saints
and all of creation to honour and exalt you.

Grant us, Lord, **your servant heart. Amen.**

The Creed

Let us stand to say the Creed:

**We believe in one God,
the Father, the Almighty,
maker of heaven and earth,
of all that is,
seen and unseen.**

**We believe in one Lord, Jesus Christ,
the only Son of God,
eternally begotten of the Father,
God from God, Light from Light,
true God from true God,
begotten, not made,
of one Being with the Father;
through him all things were made.
For us and for our salvation
he came down from heaven,
was incarnate from the Holy Spirit
and the Virgin Mary
and was made man.
For our sake he was crucified under Pontius Pilate;
he suffered death and was buried.
On the third day he rose again
in accordance with the Scriptures;
he ascended into heaven
and is seated at the right hand of the Father.
He will come again in glory
to judge the living and the dead,
and his kingdom will have no end.**

**We believe in the Holy Spirit,
the Lord, the giver of life,
who proceeds from the Father and the Son,
who with the Father and the Son
is worshipped and glorified,
who has spoken through the prophets.
We believe in one holy, catholic and apostolic Church.
We acknowledge one baptism
for the forgiveness of sins.
We look for the resurrection of the dead,
and the life of the world to come. Amen.**

10 *The Peace*

Once we were far off,
but now in union with Christ Jesus
we have been brought near
through the shedding of Christ's blood,
for he is our peace.

Encourage the congregation to share the Peace with one another in the centre of the circle.

The peace of the Lord be always with you
and also with you.
Let us offer one another a sign of peace.

All may exchange a sign of peace.

All may sit.

Song to minister At the foot of the cross (*The Source*)

11 *The Eucharistic Prayer (A)*

The Lord is here.
His Spirit is with us.

Lift up your hearts.
We lift them to the Lord.

Let us give thanks to the Lord our God.
It is right to give thanks and praise.

It is indeed right,
it is our duty and our joy,
at all times and in all places
to give you thanks and praise,
holy Father, heavenly King,
almighty and eternal God,
through Jesus Christ your Son our Lord.

And now we give you thanks
because, for our salvation,
he was obedient even to death on the cross.
The tree of shame was made the tree of glory;
and where life was lost, there life has been restored.

Therefore with angels and archangels,
and with all the company of heaven,
we proclaim your great and glorious name,
for ever praising you and *saying*:

**Holy, holy, holy Lord,
God of power and might,
heaven and earth are full of your glory.
Hosanna in the highest.**

Accept our praises, heavenly Father,
through your Son our Saviour Jesus Christ,
and as we follow his example and obey his command,
grant that by the power of your Holy Spirit
these gifts of bread and wine
may be to us his body and his blood;

who, in the same night that he was betrayed,
took bread and gave you thanks;
he broke it and gave it to his disciples, saying:
Take, eat; this is my body which is given for you;
do this in remembrance of me.

To you be glory and praise for ever.

In the same way, after supper
he took the cup and gave you thanks;
he gave it to them saying:

This song should be sung for the congregation to help prepare their hearts for Communion. Encourage them to meditate on the words.

Drink this, all of you;
this is my blood of the new covenant,
which is shed for you and for many
for the forgiveness of sins.
Do this, as often as you drink it,
in remembrance of me.

To you be glory and praise for ever.

Therefore, heavenly Father,
we remember his offering of himself
made once for all upon the cross;
we proclaim his mighty resurrection
and glorious ascension;
we look for the coming of your kingdom,
and with this bread and this cup
we make the memorial of Christ your Son our Lord.

Jesus Christ is Lord:
**Lord, by your cross and resurrection
you have set us free.
You are the Saviour of the world.**

Accept through him, our great high priest,
this our sacrifice of thanks and praise,
and as we eat and drink these holy gifts
in the presence of your divine majesty,
renew us by your Spirit,
inspire us with your love
and unite us in the body of your Son,
Jesus Christ our Lord.

To you be glory and praise for ever.

Through him, and with him, and in him,
in the unity of the Holy Spirit,
with all who stand before you in earth and heaven,
we worship you, Father almighty,
in songs of everlasting praise:

**Blessing and honour and glory and power
be yours for ever and ever. Amen.**

12   *The Lord's Prayer*

Let us pray for the coming of God's kingdom in the
words our Saviour taught us.
**Our Father in heaven,
hallowed be your name,
your kingdom come,
your will be done,
on earth as in heaven.
Give us today our daily bread.
Forgive us our sins
as we forgive those who sin against us.
Lead us not into temptation
but deliver us from evil.
For the kingdom, the power,
and the glory are yours
now and for ever. Amen.**

13   *Breaking of the Bread*

The president breaks the consecrated bread.
Come, take this bread, this is his body.
Eat and think of him, this is our saving grace.
Take, this his cup, blood shed for many.
Drink and think of him, this is our saving grace.

**We do not presume
to come to this your table, merciful Lord,
trusting in our own righteousness,
but in your manifold and great mercies.
We are not worthy
so much as to gather up the crumbs under your table.
But you are the same Lord
whose nature is always to have mercy.
Grant us, therefore, gracious Lord,
so to eat the flesh of your dear Son Jesus Christ
and to drink his blood,
that our sinful bodies may be made clean by his body
and our souls washed through his most precious blood,
and that we may evermore dwell in him, and he in us.
Amen.**

The president and people receive Communion.

> Encourage the congregation to approach the table informally, kneel if possible and offer one another Communion. Enough cups and plates should be used so that people are not lingering too long. Prayer ministry could be available.

Songs   What kind of love is this (*The Source*)
How deep the Father's love for us (*The Source*)
Here is love (*The Source*)

> Sung worship should be gentle and sensitive. Perhaps solo singing would be appropriate. Instrumental music linking the songs would be effective and help create an environment of reflection and prayer. Towards the conclusion of Communion the music ends.

14   *Silence*

15   *Prayer after Communion*

Lord Jesus Christ,
you humbled yourself in taking the form of a servant,
and in obedience died on the cross for our salvation:
give us the mind to follow you
and to proclaim you as Lord and King,
to the glory of God the Father.

**Almighty God,
we thank you for feeding us
with the body and blood of your Son Jesus Christ.
Through him we offer you our souls and bodies
to be a living sacrifice.
Send us out in the power of your Spirit
to live and work to your praise and glory. Amen.**

> Before the Blessing offer the opportunity for prayer after the service. Perhaps the worship highlighted a need for response, healing or advice.

16   *The Blessing and Dismissal*

The Lord bless you and keep you;
the Lord make his face shine upon you
and be gracious to you;
the Lord turn his face toward you
and give you peace. (Numbers 6:24-26)

Go in peace to love and serve the Lord.
In the name of Christ. Amen.

17   *Prayer Ministry*

(Continues as needed)

Soft worship music could be played as people leave and whilst prayer continues.

The Day of Pentecost – Service of Holy Communion
Theme: Filled with the Spirit

Order of Service

1 Welcome and Notices

2 Introduction to the Theme

3 Acclamation
Stand

> The love of God has been poured into our hearts
> through the Holy Spirit who has been given to us:
> **we dwell in him and he in us.**

> Give thanks to the Lord and call upon his name:
> **make known his deeds among the peoples.**

> Sing to him, sing praises to him:
> **and speak of all his marvellous works.**

> Holy, holy, holy, is the Lord God almighty:
> **who was and is and is to come!**

**4 Extended Time of Sung Worship
(taking in Confession)**

Hymn Holy, Holy, Holy! (*The Source*) or
Song Praise God from whom all blessings flow
　　　(*The Source*)
Song As we seek your face (*The Source*)

5 Open Worship

> (Open to God, open prayer or praise, reflecting,
> sharing gifts)

6 Silence

7 Preparation and Confession

> Let us sit or kneel to pray together:
> **Almighty God,**
> **to whom all hearts are open,**
> **all desires known,**
> **and from whom no secrets are hidden:**
> **cleanse the thoughts of our hearts**
> **by the inspiration of your Holy Spirit,**
> **that we may perfectly love you,**
> **and worthily magnify your holy name;**
> **through Christ our Lord. Amen.**

Remain seated.

Hymn Breathe on me, Breath of God (verses 1 and 2)
　　　(*The Source*)

Directions

Warm and inviting. Visitors and newcomers
should be made particularly welcome.

SHORT PAUSE

Read Acclamation without announcing it.
As Acclamation starts, extended
introduction to hymn or song begins
softly in background.

Move directly into sung worship.

Play soft instrumental music in background.
Open to the Holy Spirit. The congregation
may be encouraged to reflect, pray quietly
or out loud and share gifts of the Spirit. It
is important for the leader of the worship
to direct sensitively at this point.

The music ends.

Introduction to the hymn begins
unannounced.

Holy, holy, holy is the Lord almighty;
the whole earth is full of his glory.
As we too look upon the Lord we cry with Isaiah,
'Woe to me! I am ruined,
for I am a person of unclean lips
and I live among a people of unclean lips
and my eyes have seen the King, the Lord almighty.'
Spirit of God we need you to cleanse us,
to make clean our lips and sweep away our sin,
to breathe new life in us.
We lift our eyes to you, Lord,
and confess the burden of our hearts.

O King enthroned on high,
filling the earth with your glory:
holy is your name,
Lord God almighty.
In our sinfulness we cry to you
to take our guilt away,
and to cleanse our lips to speak your word,
through Jesus Christ our Lord. Amen.

May the Father forgive *us*
by the death of his Son
and strengthen *us*
to live in the power of the Spirit
all *our* days. **Amen.**

Hymn Breathe on me, Breath of God (verses 3 and 4)

Collect
God, who at this time
taught the hearts of your faithful people
by sending to them the light of your Holy Spirit:
grant us by the same Spirit
to have a right judgement in all things
and evermore to rejoice in his holy comfort;
through the merits of Christ Jesus our Saviour,
who is alive and reigns with you,
in the unity of the Holy Spirit,
one God, now and for ever.

8   *The Liturgy of the Word*
Reading 1
Short time of silence

Reading 2
Short time of silence

Sermon

9   *Silence*

Instrumental music of the hymn continues softly in the background.

Towards the conclusion of the Absolution the instrumental music leads into an extended intro to the hymn.

Verses 3 and 4 should build musically to encourage affirmation of forgiveness and new start.

SHORT PAUSE

Photograph slide or image of 'a ship's sail' or 'flames' could be projected onto screen during the readings.

(Visual images off)

Sermon linked to theme. Challenging and affirming, giving practical help for life of discipleship filled with the Holy Spirit.

Silence for personal reflection on Sermon. How does God want me to respond?

10 *Prayers*

Fill us, Lord – with your Holy Spirit.
May our hearts overflow with thanks,
may our lips sing your praise
and may our lives be renewed with your breath of life.

Silence

We pray:
Holy Spirit, come.

Grant us, Lord – the gifts of your Spirit
that you so desire to pour in us.
Give us the courage and the faith
to receive them gladly and to be released
into new depths of life – life with you.

Silence

Work through our lives and our church in power
so that others may be touched with your love,
and hearts may be won for your kingdom;
all to the glory of your name.

We pray:
Holy Spirit, come.

Awaken us, Lord – to see your purposes and your ways.
Holy Spirit, you are the life-giver
and we love to see you at work within creation
and the world in which we live.
As a nation we are in such need
of your power and love.
Breathe new life into the dry bones of faith,
pour living water to quench our thirst for you
and flood this land with hope and healing love.

Silence

We pray:
Holy Spirit, come.

Move, Lord Jesus – within our own community.
Through your saving love reach out to the lost,
the broken and the fallen.
Help us to be your voice calling to those in need
and your hands ministering support and care.
We lift to you now those in need of your healing Spirit
because of sickness and suffering.

Silence

We pray:
Holy Spirit, come.

On this occasion the prayers follow the sermon so that 'prayer' is a direct response to conclude the Liturgy of the Word. Prayers are unannounced and follow time of silence.

Thank you, heavenly Father – that through your Son
you have given us the gift of eternal life.
Set this hope in our hearts so that each day
we will live to bring you praise and glory.
Unite your church to be one in heart and mind
so that together we will pray . . .

Holy Spirit, come.

Song Holy Spirit come (*The Source*)

The Creed

Let us stand to say the Creed:
We believe in one God,
the Father, the almighty,
maker of heaven and earth,
of all that is,
seen and unseen.

We believe in one Lord, Jesus Christ,
the only Son of God,
eternally begotten of the Father,
God from God, Light from Light
true God from true God,
begotten, not made,
of one Being with the Father.
Through him all things were made.
For us and for our salvation
he came down from heaven;
by the power of the Holy Spirit
he became incarnate of the Virgin Mary,
and was made man.
For our sake he was crucified under Pontius Pilate;
he suffered death and was buried.
On the third day he rose again
in accordance with the scriptures;
he ascended into heaven
and is seated at the right hand of the Father.
he will come again in glory
to judge the living and the dead,
and his kingdom will have no end.

We believe in the Holy Spirit,
the Lord, the giver of life,
who proceeds from the Father and the Son.
With the Father and the Son
he is worshipped and glorified.
He has spoken through the Prophets.

We believe in one holy, catholic and apostolic Church.
We acknowledge one baptism for the forgiveness of sins.
We look for the resurrection of the dead,
and the life of the world to come. Amen.

Instrumental introduction to song begins
softly in the background.

Song begins unannounced. Sing gently.
Music could continue afterwards whilst
people pray or sit quietly.
Music ends before the Creed.

11   *The Peace*

God has made us one in Christ.
He has set his seal upon us and,
as a pledge of what is to come,
has given the Spirit to dwell in our hearts. Alleluia.

The peace of the Lord be always with you
and also with you.
Let us offer one another a sign of peace.

All may exchange a sign of peace.

12   *The Eucharistic Prayer (B)*

The Lord is here.
His Spirit is with us.

Lift up your hearts.
We lift them to the Lord.

Let us give thanks to the Lord our God.
It is right to give thanks and praise.

It is indeed right, it is our duty and our joy,
always and everywhere to give you thanks,
holy Father, almighty and everlasting God,
through Jesus Christ, your only Son our Lord.
This day we give you thanks
because in fulfilment of your promise
you pour out your Spirit upon us,
filling us with your gifts, leading us into all truth,
and uniting peoples of many tongues
in the confession of one faith.
Your Spirit gives us grace to call you Father,
to proclaim your gospel to all nations
and to serve you as a royal priesthood.
Therefore we join our voices
with angels and archangels,
and with all those in whom the Spirit dwells,
to proclaim the glory of your name,
for ever praising you and saying:

Holy, holy, holy Lord,
God of power and might,
heaven and earth are full of your glory.
Hosanna in the highest.

Lord, you are holy indeed, the source of all holiness;
grant that by the power of your Holy Spirit,
and according to your holy will,
these gifts of bread and wine
may be to us the body and blood
of our Lord Jesus Christ;

who, in the same night that he was betrayed,
took bread and gave you thanks;
he broke it and gave it to his disciples, saying:
Take, eat; this is my body which is given for you;
do this in remembrance of me.

Before the Eucharistic prayer begins explain to the congregation that during Communion an anointing with oil will be available. Explain that oil is a symbol of the Holy Spirit and by being anointed you are expressing your desire to be filled with the Spirit of God, his life-giving power. People may wish to renew their life with the Lord, may wish to ask for healing or to ask for a specific gift of the Spirit. Whatever the reason, encourage them to go forward to receive Communion and then go to the appropriate area in the church given over for this particular time of ministry.

A trained prayer or ministry team will be needed to administer the oil (a simple sign of the cross on the forehead in the name of the Father, Son and Holy Spirit) and to pray with each person with the laying on of hands.

In the same way, after supper
he took the cup and gave you thanks;
he gave it to them, saying;
Drink this, all of you;
this is my blood of the new covenant,
which is shed for you and for many
for the forgiveness of sins.
Do this, as often as you drink it,
In remembrance of me.

Great is the mystery of faith:
Christ has died:
Christ is risen:
Christ will come again.

And so, Father, calling to mind his death on the cross,
his perfect sacrifice made once
for the sins of the whole world;
rejoicing in his mighty resurrection
and glorious ascension,
and looking for his coming in glory,
we celebrate this memorial of our redemption.
As we offer you this our sacrifice
of praise and thanksgiving,
we bring before you this bread and this cup
and we thank you for counting us worthy
to stand in your presence and serve you.

Send the Holy Spirit on your people
and gather into one in your kingdom
all who share this one bread and one cup,
so that we, in the company of (*N and*) all the saints,
may praise and glorify you for ever,
through Jesus Christ our Lord;

by whom, and with whom, and in whom,
in the unity of the Holy Spirit,
all honour and glory be yours, almighty Father,
for ever and ever. **Amen.**

13   *The Lord's Prayer*

Let us sit or kneel to pray for the coming of God's
kingdom in the words our Saviour taught us:

Our Father in heaven,
hallowed be your name,
your kingdom come,
your will be done,
on earth as in heaven.
Give us today our daily bread.
Forgive us our sins
as we forgive those who sin against us.
Lead us not into temptation
but deliver us from evil.
For the kingdom, the power,
and the glory are yours
now and for ever. Amen.

14 *Breaking of the Bread*

The president breaks the consecrated bread.
We break this bread to share in the body of Christ.
**Though we are many, we are one body,
because we all share in one bread.**

15 *Giving of Communion*

Alleluia. Christ our Passover is sacrificed for us.
Therefore let us keep the feast. Alleluia.

Songs By his grace (*The Source*)
The Spirit of the Lord (*The Source 2*)
Holy Spirit, come (*The Source*)

16 *Silence*

17 *Prayer after Communion*

Faithful God,
who fulfilled the promises of Easter
by sending us your Holy Spirit
and opening to every race and nation
the way of life eternal:
open our lips by your Spirit,
that every tongue may tell of your glory;
through Jesus Christ our Lord. **Amen.**

**Almighty God,
we thank you for feeding us
with the body and blood of your Son Jesus Christ.
Through him we offer you our souls and bodies
to be a living sacrifice.
Send us out in the power of your Spirit
to live and work to your praise and glory. Amen.**

Song There is a Redeemer (*The Source*)

18 *The Blessing and Dismissal*

May Christ's holy, healing, enabling Spirit be with you
and guide you on your way at every change and turn.

And the blessing of God almighty,
the Father, the Son and the Holy Spirit,
be among you and remain with you always.

Go in peace to love and serve the Lord.
In the name of Christ. Amen.

Anointing with oil and prayer ministry. Singing and music must be soft and sensitive during combined Communion and prayer ministry. The songs could be linked to form an extended time of sung worship.

Music ends.

After Communion the service continues whilst people continue to receive prayer ministry.

Before the singing of the Grace offer the opportunity for prayer or anointing with oil after the service. Maybe people felt unable to respond earlier but would like to now.

19   ***The Grace*** (sung) (*The Source 2*)

  **The grace of our Lord Jesus Christ
and the love of God
and the fellowship of the Holy Spirit
be with us for evermore.**

20   ***Prayer Ministry***

  (Continues as needed)

Soft worship music could be played as people leave or as prayer continues.

Fourth Sunday after Trinity – Service of the Word
Theme: Worship Jesus first, with everything!

Preparation

The following are the simple guidelines for the visual elements suggested for this service. To be effective they must be done well and thoroughly. A gifted artist within the congregation could be employed for these tasks. When done imaginatively these visual and experiential aspects of worship can have great impact. However, worship is not dependent on such things and you may wish to keep things simple or to be open and 'go with the flow' of worship on the day.

A large wooden cross could be displayed artistically at the front of church. At the cross, roses should be placed (artificial or real). Baskets of scented rose petals could be placed around the church (with enough petals for each person present). Incense or essential oils could be burned around the church to help create the impression of a fragrant offering to the Lord.

Order of Service

1 Welcome and Notices

2 Introduction to the Theme

3 Opening Prayer and Extended Time of Sung Worship

> We pray together:
>
> **Loving Lord,**
> **fill us with your life-giving,**
> **joy-giving, peace-giving presence,**
> **that we may praise you now with our lips**
> **and all the day long with our lives,**
> **through Jesus Christ our Lord. Amen.**

> *Stand*
>
> **Hymn** O worship the King (*The Source*) or
> **Song** I will praise you my God and King
>   (*Release – High Above the Nations*)
> **Song** Come, now is the time to worship (*The Bridge*)
> **Song** Jesus, all for Jesus (*The Source 2*)

4 Open Worship

> (Open to God, open prayer or praise, reflecting, sharing gifts)

5 Silence

6 Confession

> **Song** From heaven you came (verses 1, 2 and 3)
>   (*The Source*)

Directions

Warm and inviting. Visitors and newcomers should be made particularly welcome.

SHORT PAUSE

Introduce prayer without announcing it.

Introduction to hymn or song immediately after the prayer (unannounced).

Three songs linked together with instrumental music.

Soft instrumental music continues during Open Worship.
As and when appropriate the music ends.

After the silence the congregation should again be able to pray quietly or out loud, speak out praise or share how God has encouraged them. Leader may conclude this section of worship with a prayer.

Introduction to the song begins unannounced.

Let us then approach the throne of grace with confidence, so that we may receive mercy and find grace to help us in our time of need.
We sit or kneel to pray:

Lord our God,
in our sin we have avoided your call.
Our love for you is like a morning cloud,
like the dew that goes away early.
Have mercy on us;
deliver us from judgement;
bind up our wounds
and revive us;
in Jesus Christ our Lord. Amen.

Song From heaven you came (verse 4) (*The Source*)

Collect
O God, the protector of all who trust in you,
without whom nothing is strong, nothing is holy:
increase and multiply upon us your mercy;
that with you as our ruler and guide
we may so pass through things temporal
that we lose not our hold on things eternal;
grant this, heavenly Father,
for our Lord Jesus Christ's sake,
who is alive and reigns with you,
in the unity of the Holy Spirit,
one God, now and for ever.

7   *The Liturgy of the Word*
Reading 1
Short time of silence

Reading 2
Short time of silence

Sermon

8   *Silence*

9   *Response*

Private worship offering (sitting or kneeling quietly)

or

Practical worship offering by kneeling at the cross and placing petal on the cross.

Image of cupped hands and water projected on screen.
Soft instrumental music continues in background during invitation.

PAUSE
Image off.
Instrumental music continues.

Music moves into introduction for the final verse of the song.

Music ends.
Image of cupped hands and water returns to the screen.

Image off.

No announcement of the readings – should be unbroken time of listening and reflecting.

Sermon linked to theme and readings. Challenging and affirming, giving teaching on worship and our loving response to Jesus – drawing close enough to kiss (intimacy), kneeling at God's feet (the feet that walked the path to the cross).

For reflection on the Sermon.

Soft instrumental music of the next song played in background.
Baskets of rose petals to be passed along each row. Congregation invited to take a petal, hold it in their hands and enjoy its fragrance. They are then invited to look at the cross at the front of church and to consider how they should worship Jesus at this moment. Each can give their fragrant offering to the Lord as a way of giving him everything and drawing close enough to worship at his feet. Then invite them either to sit and give offerings privately in their hearts or to come forward, kneel at the cross and lay their offering there.

Song I will offer up my life (*The Source*) or
I give you all the honour (*The Source*)

10 *Open Worship*

(Sharing gifts of the Spirit, open prayer, praise or
testimony)
or
Silence

11 *Prayers*

Lord, as we kneel at your feet
receive our heartfelt worship.
May it be a pleasing and fragrant offering only for you.
As sinners we are unfit to draw near
and yet you welcome and embrace us
because your compassion is without end
and you are so eager to forgive.
Our love can never match the love you show
but still we give all we have.
May all our lives be to you
an offering of thanks and praise
so that you alone are glorified above all things.

Silence

Lord, trusting in your love
we give you our prayer.

Lord, we bring before you the world in which we live.
You see the violence, the suffering, the hatred,
the destruction and injustice – your heart must grieve.
As Lord of all we trust that you will continue
to pour your living waters into this thirsty world
so that violence gives way to peace,
suffering turns to healing,
destruction gives way to growth
and injustice makes way for truth and fairness.
Grant wisdom and humility to all our leaders
so that strengthened and guided
by your life-changing power
they may work through any situation
in accordance with your will.

Silence

Lord, trusting in your love
we give you our prayer.

Lord, we give to you our own community,
its character, strengths and weaknesses.
We thank you for our homes and neighbours
and ask that you would bless them with your Spirit.
We lift to you the vulnerable members of the community
and ask that, empowered by you,
we might show them your love and compassion.
May this church be a place of refreshment and refuge
for the weary or the broken
and may we shine as a bright star leading people to you.

Music moves into songs during response.

After Response and Worship, instrumental music could continue whilst people pray or express their worship more freely. If you haven't provided a response so far you may feel led to encourage the congregation or to lead them in a heartfelt response. It is important for the leader to be open to the Holy Spirit and flexible.

After worship and response, prayers follow on immediately without announcement. Music ends.

You may wish to play in the background a recording of classical or other music suitable to an environment of prayer.

Silence

Lord, trusting in your love
we give you our prayer.

Lord, we bring before you the sick,
the suffering and those in need.
You have power over all things
and we ask you to heal, comfort and provide
for the people we lift to you now . . .

Silence

Lord Jesus, fill us with your compassion
so that we might reach out to those who need us
and spark fresh hope into their lives.

Lord, trusting in your love
we give you our prayer.

Lord, we give you our thanks.
You have shown us such grace and given us true hope.
You are the one true King who deserves our offerings
of worship and love before and above all things.
Together with all the saints, heavenly hosts
and all of creation
we will proclaim how great you are.

Lord, trusting in your love
we give you our prayer. Amen.

Let us now pray for the coming of God's kingdom
using the words our Lord Jesus Christ told us:

Our Father in heaven,
hallowed be your name,
your kingdom come,
your will be done,
on earth as in heaven.
Give us today our daily bread.
Forgive us our sins
as we forgive those who sin against us.
Lead us not into temptation
but deliver us from evil.
For the kingdom, the power,
and the glory are yours
now and for ever. Amen.

Stand

Song My Jesus, my Saviour (*The Source*)

Instrumental music to the next song begins as the Lord's Prayer starts and builds towards the introduction on the words 'For the kingdom'

The song flows naturally from the Lord's Prayer unannounced.

PAUSE

Let us declare our faith in God:
**We believe in God the Father,
from whom every family
in heaven and on earth is named.**

**We believe in God the Son,
who lives in our hearts through faith,
and fills us with his love.**

**We believe in God the Holy Spirit,
who strengthens us
with power from on high.**

**We believe in one God;
Father, Son and Holy Spirit. Amen.**

The introductory sentence to the belief is said unannounced.

12 *The Blessing*

Go forth into the world in peace;
be of good courage;
hold fast to that which is good;
render to no one evil for evil;
strengthen the fainthearted; support the weak;
help the afflicted; honour everyone;
love and serve the Lord,
rejoicing in the power of the Holy Spirit.
And the blessing of God almighty,
the Father, the Son and the Holy Spirit,
be among you and remain with you always.

The Blessing follows immediately after the belief.

Before the singing of the Grace offer the further opportunity for prayer after the service. Maybe people would like to make their offering to the Lord at this point as they felt unable to do so earlier. Or perhaps God is encouraging them in some way to respond to what they have heard or sensed in their hearts.

13 *The Grace* (sung) (*The Source 2*)

**The grace of our Lord Jesus Christ
and the love of God
and the fellowship of the Holy Spirit
be with us for evermore.**

14 *Prayer Ministry Available*

Gentle worship music could continue as people leave and as prayer continues.

Seventeenth Sunday after Trinity
Optional theme – Service of Holy Communion

Order of Service

1 Grace, mercy and peace
from God our Father
and the Lord Jesus Christ
be with you
and also with you.

2 *Welcome and Notices*

3 *Extended Time of Sung Worship*
Stand
Hymn Tell out, my soul (*The Source*) or
Song Let everything that has breath praise the Lord
(*The Bridge*)
Song Faithful One (*The Source*)
Song Father, we love you (*The Source*)

4 *Open Worship*
(Open to God, open prayer or praise, reflecting,
sharing gifts)

5 *Silence*

6 *Preparation and Confession*
Let us sit or kneel as we pray together:
Almighty God,
to whom all hearts are open,
all desires known,
and from whom no secrets are hidden:
cleanse the thoughts of our hearts
by the inspiration of your Holy Spirit,
that we may perfectly love you,
and worthily magnify your holy name;
through Christ our Lord. Amen.

God so loved the world
that he gave his only Son Jesus Christ
to save us from our sins,
to be our advocate in heaven,
and to bring us to eternal life.

Directions

Warm and inviting. Visitors and newcomers
should be made particularly welcome.
SHORT PAUSE

Soft instrumental music played in
background.
Open to the Holy Spirit.
The congregation may be encouraged to
reflect, pray quietly or out loud and share
gifts of the Spirit. It is important for the
worship leader to direct sensitively at this
point. The music then ends softly.

After the time of silence you may wish to
ask if anyone would like to share some
thoughts or testimony with the congregation.
Alternatively you may wish to conclude this
section with an appropriate prayer.

As the invitation to Confession starts,
instrumental music to the song 'Before the
throne of God' plays softly in the background
and continues through the Confession.

Let us confess our sins in penitence and faith,
firmly resolved to keep God's commandments
and to live in love and peace with all.

Almighty God, our heavenly Father,
we have sinned against you
and against our neighbour
in thought and word and deed,
through negligence, through weakness,
through our own deliberate fault.
We are truly sorry
and repent of all our sins.
For the sake of your Son Jesus Christ,
who died for us,
forgive us all that is past,
and grant that we may serve you in newness of life
to the glory of your name.
Amen.

Almighty God,
who forgives all who truly repent,
have mercy upon *you*,
pardon and deliver *you* from all *your* sins,
confirm and strengthen *you* in all goodness,
and keep *you* in life eternal;
through Jesus Christ our Lord.
Amen.

Stand

Song Before the throne of God above (*The Source 2*)

7   *Silence*

Almighty God,
you have made us for yourself,
and our hearts are restless till they find their rest in you:
pour your love into our hearts and draw us to yourself,
and so bring us at last to your heavenly city
where we shall see you face to face;
through Jesus Christ, your Son our Lord,
who is alive and reigns with you,
in the unity of the Holy Spirit,
one God, now and for ever. Amen.

8   *The Liturgy of the Word*

Sit

Reading 1
Short time of silence

Reading 2
Short time of silence

Sermon

Towards the conclusion of the Absolution
the instrumental music leads into an
extended introduction to the song 'Before
the throne of God above'.

After the song the music ends.

SHORT PAUSE

9 *Period of Silence and Response*

A song of response could be included here. Alternatively an extended time of sung worship.

The Creed

Let us stand to say the Creed:

**We believe in one God,
the Father, the Almighty,
maker of heaven and earth,
of all that is,
seen and unseen.**

**We believe in one Lord, Jesus Christ,
the only Son of God,
eternally begotten of the Father,
God from God, Light from Light,
true God from true God,
begotten, not made,
of one Being with the Father;
through him all things were made.
For us and for our salvation
he came down from heaven,
was incarnate from the Holy Spirit
and of the Virgin Mary
and was made man.
For our sake he was crucified under Pontius Pilate;
he suffered death and was buried.
On the third day he rose again
in accordance with the Scriptures;
he ascended into heaven
and is seated at the right hand of the Father.
He will come again in glory
to judge the living and the dead,
and his kingdom will have no end.**

**We believe in the Holy Spirit,
the Lord, the giver of life,
who proceeds from the Father and the Son,
who with the Father and the Son
is worshipped and glorified,
who has spoken through the prophets.
We believe in one holy catholic and apostolic Church.
We acknowledge one baptism
for the forgiveness of sins.
We look for the resurrection of the dead,
and the life of the world to come. Amen.**

Please sit to pray.

10 *Visual Prayer*

For personal reflection and response to Sermon. How does God want each of us to respond? Maybe guide people's prayers as an opportunity for response.

Background music begins.

Explain to the congregation how this form of prayer works – they will see images and headings to guide their prayers, each new subject will be introduced briefly.
Use projected headings and images as the guidelines for prayer. Atmospheric background music and spoken introductions to each heading could also be used.
Preparation: During the week prior to the service collect newspaper headlines and pictures to use as prayer headings and stimuli. Cut and paste them onto white A4 paper and photocopy onto OHP acetates.

Merciful Father,
accept these prayers
for the sake of your Son,
our Saviour Jesus Christ,
Amen.

11   *The Liturgy of the Sacrament*
The Peace

Blessed are the peacemakers:
they shall be called children of God.
We meet in the name of Christ and share his peace.

The peace of the Lord be always with you
and also with you.
Let us offer one another a sign of peace.

All may exchange a sign of peace.

If the gifts of the people are presented this prayer may be
said:

Yours, Lord, is the greatness, the power,
the glory, the splendour and the majesty;
for everything in heaven and on earth is yours.
All things come from you,
and of your own do we give you.

12   *The Eucharistic Prayer (D)*

The Lord be with you
and also with you.

Lift up your hearts.
We lift them to the Lord.

Let us give thanks to the Lord our God.
It is right to give thanks and praise.

Almighty God, good Father to us all,
your face is turned towards your world.
In love you gave us Jesus your Son
to rescue us from sin and death.
Your Word goes out to call us home
to the city where angels sing your praise.
We join with them in heaven's song:

Holy, holy, holy Lord,
God of power and might,
heaven and earth are full of your glory.
Hosanna in the highest.

Father of all, we give you thanks
for every gift that comes from heaven.

To the darkness Jesus came as your light.
With signs of faith and words of hope
he touched untouchables with love
and washed the guilty clean.

Add to this collection other appropriate
headings or images you would like to use.
These will form the basis for the prayer
time. Select some appropriate music to be
played in the background. In addition,
video material taken from the week's news
could be used in conjunction with the OHP.
Alternatively images and video clips can be
imported into a *Powerpoint* presentation to
be used with computer and data projector.

This is his story.
This is our song:
Hosanna in the highest.

The crowds came out to see your Son,
yet at the end they turned on him.
On the night he was betrayed
he came to table with his friends
to celebrate the freedom of your people.

This is his story.
This is our song:
Hosanna in the highest.

Jesus blessed you, Father, for the food;
he took bread, gave thanks, broke it and said:
This is my body, given for you all.
Jesus then gave thanks for the wine;
he took the cup, gave it and said:
This is my blood, shed for you all
for the forgiveness of sins.
Do this in remembrance of me.

This is our story.
This is our song:
Hosanna in the highest.

Therefore, Father, with this bread and this cup
we celebrate the cross
on which he died to set us free.
Defying death he rose again
and is alive with you to plead for us and all the world.

This is our story.
This is our song:
Hosanna in the highest.

Send your Spirit on us now
that by these gifts we may feed on Christ
with opened eyes and hearts on fire.

May we and all who share this food
offer ourselves to live for you
and be welcomed at your feast in heaven
where all creation worships you,
Father, Son and Holy Spirit:

Blessing and honour and glory and power
be yours for ever and ever. Amen.

13   *The Lord's Prayer*

Let us sit or kneel to pray for the coming of God's
kingdom in the words our Saviour taught us:

Our Father in heaven,
hallowed be your name,
your kingdom come,
your will be done,
on earth as in heaven.
Give us today our daily bread.
Forgive us our sins
as we forgive those who sin against us.

**Lead us not into temptation
but deliver us from evil.
For the kingdom, the power,
and the glory are yours
now and for ever. Amen.**

14 *Breaking of the Bread*

The president breaks the consecrated bread.

We break this bread to share in the body of Christ.
**Though we are many, we are one body,
because we all share in one bread.**

15 *Giving of Communion*

Draw near with faith.
Receive the body of our Lord Jesus Christ
which he gave for you,
and his blood which he shed for you.
Eat and drink
in remembrance that he died for you,
and feed on him in your hearts
by faith with thanksgiving.

Songs How deep the Father's love for us (*The Source*)
Father, you are my portion (*The Source*)
Father, I come to you (*The Source*)

16 *Silence*

17 *Prayer after Communion*

Lord, we pray that your grace
may always precede and follow us,
and make us continually to be given to all good works;
through Jesus Christ our Lord. **Amen.**

**Father of all,
we give you thanks and praise,
that when we were still far off
you met us in your Son and brought us home.
Dying and living, he declared your love,
gave us grace, and opened the gate of glory.
May we who share Christ's body live his risen life;
we who drink his cup bring life to others;
we whom the Spirit lights give light to the world.
Keep us firm in the hope you have set before us,
so we and all your children shall be free,
and the whole earth live to praise your name;
through Christ our Lord.
Amen.**

Stand

Song Salvation belongs to our God (*The Source*)

Music introduction to the approaching song begins softly and builds during the prayer.

After the Amen the introduction immediately leads into the song.

Before the Blessing and Dismissal offer prayer ministry.

18 *The Blessing and Dismissal*

The peace of God,
which passes all understanding,
keep your hearts and minds
in the knowledge and love of God,
and of his Son Jesus Christ our Lord;
and the blessing of God almighty,
the Father, the Son, and the Holy Spirit,
be among you and remain with you always.
Amen.

Go in peace to love and serve the Lord.
In the name of Christ. Amen.

19 *Prayer Ministry Available*

Soft worship music could be played as people leave or as prayer continues.

A service exploring freedom in worship — Service of the Word

Order of Service

1 Gathering Worship

2 Welcome and Notices

3 Introduction to the Service

4 Extended Time of Sung Worship
Stand
Songs Great is the Lord (*The Source*)
    Lord, I lift your name on high (*The Source*)
    Father of creation (*The Source*)

5 Open Worship
(Open to God, open prayer or praise, reflecting, sharing gifts)

6 Silence

7 Sharing

Sit if not doing so already.

8 Confession
Here is love (verse 1) (*The Source*)

Jesus is our high priest, tempted like us, yet without sin. He lives for ever in heaven to intercede for us. Through him we approach the throne of grace with confidence, and confess our sins.

**My God, for love of you
I desire to hate and forsake all sins
by which I have ever displeased you;
and I resolve by the help of your grace
to commit them no more;
and to avoid all opportunities of sin.
Help me to do this,
through Jesus Christ our Lord. Amen.**

Here is love (verse 2)

Directions

Whilst people enter. Sung by music group or band. Includes new songs to be sung during the service and songs reflecting a call to worship. Drinks and doughnuts served as people gather.

Warm and inviting. Visitors and newcomers should be made particularly welcome.

Brief background into the area you hope to explore today. May conclude with a prayer asking God to accomplish his purpose amongst you as you seek him and worship him.

Move directly into extended time of sung worship. Three songs should be linked together with instrumental music.

Open to the Spirit. Instrumental music continues, worship leader may direct appropriate response – pray quietly, speak out praise, concluding prayer, pray out loud or singing in the Spirit.

Music ends. If not said already say concluding prayer.

Give members of congregation opportunity to share a testimony, any words of knowledge, pictures, etc.

SHORT PAUSE
After the pause, begin introduction to 'Here is love' (verse 1).

Instrumental music continues gently in background as introduction to Confession is said and as Confession is prayed.

After prayer, music leads into introduction to verse 2. Music builds.

May the Father of all mercies
cleanse *us* from *our* sins,
and restore *us* in his service
to the praise and glory of his name,
through Jesus Christ our Lord. **Amen.**

9 *The Liturgy of the Word*

Reading Luke 7:36-50
Short time of silence

Sermon

10 *Sung Worship and Response*

Songs When the music fades (*The Source*)
      Lord, you have my heart (*The Source*)
      Lord, you are so precious to me (*The Source*)

11 *Time of Prayer*

Let us now pray for the coming of God's kingdom
using the words our Lord Jesus Christ told us:

Our Father in heaven,
hallowed be your name,
your kingdom come,
your will be done,
on earth as in heaven.
Give us today our daily bread.
Forgive us our sins
as we forgive those who sin against us.
Lead us not into temptation
but deliver us from evil.
For the kingdom, the power,
and the glory are yours
now and for ever. Amen.

Let us stand to affirm our faith in Jesus Christ the Son
of God:

Though he was divine,
he did not cling to equality with God,
but made himself nothing.
Taking the form of a slave,
he was born in human likeness.
He humbled himself,
and was obedient to death –
even the death of the cross.
Therefore God has raised him on high,
and given him the name above every name:

Instrumental music continues during Absolution.

Music ends.

Affirming but challenging. Exploring worship at Jesus' feet – preoccupation with Jesus, expression, freedom from restrictions, sacrificial love.

Worship leader should go with the flow in order to guide worship and response. Be open to the Holy Spirit and the way people respond. Musicians be flexible! May include extended instrumentals, open prayer and space to share. May conclude with prayer said by worship leader.

Instrumental music could continue softly in background. Prayers not too long and not too rigid or dry. The person leading the prayers could have some outline plans ready but must be experienced and sufficiently competent to lead a time of prayer in response to previous time of worship. Conclude time of prayer with the Lord's Prayer.

PAUSE

that at the name of Jesus
every knee should bow,
and every voice proclaim that Jesus Christ is Lord,
to the glory of God the Father. Amen.

12 *Praise and Thanksgiving*

   Songs Jesus is the name we honour (*The Source*)
         My Jesus, my Saviour (*The Source*)

13 *Conclusion and the Grace* (*The Source 2*)

   **The grace of our Lord Jesus Christ
   and the love of God
   and the fellowship of the Holy Spirit
   be with us for evermore.**

14 *Prayer Ministry*

After Belief move directly into Praise and Thanksgiving.

Before concluding, offer prayer with the prayer ministry team after the service.

Say or sing the Grace.

Sung worship continues softly as people depart and as prayer continues.